MW01029971

The Glad

Game.

When & How
my Challenge

invite
PRESS

THE JESUS METHOD

THE JESUS METHOD

a reliable approach to navigating today's urgent social issues

TED BRYANT

invite
PRESS

Plano, Texas

DEDICATION AND ACKNOWLEDGMENT

I never want to forget what God has done for me. He not only has saved me from my sin, but he has committed to never leaving me and always refining me into the likeness of his Son. It has been so fun to journey with him in this project of discovering and sharing how he loves people so well. My brilliant wife Ang and mother of our six children is the love of my life, and her "yes" in all of this continues to demonstrate her abiding love for Jesus and constant care of our family. Our children continue to inspire me to be the husband, father, son, friend, and man that God created to me to be—I love you all so much! I am grateful to my parents, brothers, and extended family for introducing me to Jesus and modeling him in our relationships. Finally, I want to thank our church staff, especially Caryn Reynolds and the Leadership Team, for their support of this initiative. I can't believe God allows me to serve Granger Community Church. It is the honor of my life to help lead such wonderful staff, attendees, and broader Michiana community. Thank you for taking steps together toward Christ! Let's gooooo!

The Jesus Method: A Reliable Approach to Navigating Today's Urgent Social Issues

This book is printed on acid-free, elemental chlorine-free paper.

ISBN 978-1-963265-01-9

24 25 26 27 28 29 30 31 32 33 34—10 9 8 7 6 5 4 3 2 1

MANUFACTURED in the UNITED STATES of AMERICA

CONTENTS

INTRODUCTION

When I look at the world right now, I see a ton of pressurized predicaments that we face when engaging hot-topic issues in our society. I am calling these situations "social dilemmas," and there are seemingly countless ways to navigate through them. When I was writing this book, as a Christian, I wanted to know how Jesus did it. Regardless of the circumstantial storms or internal struggles that surround me, I wanted to be committed to following the way of Jesus. Unfortunately, my faith journey up to this point had not equipped me very well to navigate all the social dilemmas coming at me from every direction. In fact, I often feel paralyzed, not knowing what to do, when to do it, or how to do it, and yet, I still have a sense that I *should* be doing something!

Have you ever felt like that?

To be completely honest, I feel like the world is a mess. I want to know how Jesus handled all the social messes in his own life and ministry. With just a cursory read through the Gospels, it's obvious that Jesus's goal was not to avoid conflict or be a people pleaser. It wasn't to get the most votes or have the highest public opinion. At the same time, unlike so many religious leaders today, he didn't seem angry all the time or obsessed with getting his voice heard. He didn't need to have the last word. That makes Jesus vastly different than most of the voices in our culture today.

So, what was different about Jesus?

Yes, I know, he is the son of God, Messiah, and Savior. On the fully human side of things, though, how did he pull it off so brilliantly and without sinning? It made me wonder if the way that Jesus handled his social dilemmas could be discerned and extrapolated to help us with our own everyday social interactions.

I earnestly wanted to know how Jesus navigated the heated, disparaging, divisive, and dangerous social dilemmas that surrounded him. I had no intention of writing all this down, but after seeing the impact it had on people, I went for it. I hope that this book takes you on an adventure with God, wherever you consider yourself in faith or religion. It is often in wrestling with God that our hearts grow in proximity to Jesus. He's not afraid of our discussions, and I'm often reminded that as I share my thoughts and opinions with God, I need to also be open to receive his. This includes how Jesus wants his followers to navigate the social dilemmas in their lives. As I myself have realized, Jesus's method is clear, powerful, and challenging. Once it's understood, I believe it can affect how we navigate every relationship in our lives. Enjoy hanging out with God as you discover the Jesus Method in the pages ahead.

Social dilemma's

CHAPTER 1

CONTEXT IS KEY

A s we were coming out of the pandemic, I was spending a lot of time considering what it meant to help lead the church in our present times. It seemed like there were constant moving targets on what to address and what to leave alone. I desperately wanted to know the real, practical application of bringing the kingdom of God to Earth, right in the middle of the social dilemmas that surrounded us. That brought me to Jesus. Of course it did; I'm a Christian. But seriously, he was the best at navigating decisions like this. Adversaries often thought that they had Jesus backed into some sort of philosophical corner, and then he would brilliantly execute an unfathomable escape. He's like the Houdini of social dilemma traps. He wasn't just a teacher who offered insights for further thinking, he wasn't only an emotional catalyst, and he wasn't only someone who did a bunch of random acts of kindness. His goal wasn't only to make people feel good about themselves or to have everyone simply *think positive*. Jesus modeled perfectly what it looked like to love God with all his heart, all his mind, all his soul, and all his strength. He was the full representation of God the Father (John 14:9).

In this book, we are going to follow Jesus into the messiest social dilemmas that he faced, and here's our one goal: to learn the Jesus Method. How did he navigate all those tense situations without sinning, and what can we do to follow his method in our own social dilemmas? Whether it's politics, the economy, health care, sexuality, beginning of life, ending of a life, gender, social injustice, equality—you name it—there are plenty of social dilemmas in our culture to choose from. I'm not here to judge which ones are more important to discuss than others; I simply want us to learn the Jesus Method and then apply that in our own lives.

As I look at the world around us, it doesn't seem like we're trending toward peace and loving each other the way that Jesus loved. So many heated arguments, divisive posts, and claims of truth are swirling around. We crave to know what's right and what's wrong so that we can persevere through it all. We might even want to stand up for God or at least not appear to be ashamed of God (Luke 9:26). When Christians start to talk about all these hot topics, it often leads people to a passionate reaction like this:

> I know what's coming—we're going to talk about all the theological stances that we should have, and it doesn't matter how people are affected by that. It doesn't matter what division or anger that's going to cause. It's the truth, and they just have to deal with it. If people get angry, fine! They don't belong with us anyway. If they're hurt, well, the truth hurts sometimes. That's just the way the world is!

That's where I want step in and say, "*Exactly!*" That's exactly the way *the world* is.

Since I'm following Jesus, I'm called to a radically different way than "the world," where cultural trends of truth lead us away from

God. I'm called to only be *in* this world, not *of* this world (John 17:14–16). "That's just the way the world is" should never qualify as a justification for my reactions in social dilemmas.

Many in the Western church are trending toward a tragic trajectory. We are becoming comfortable with alienating, discarding, and even celebrating separation from the exact people that Christians were meant to reach with the love and grace of God. There is an energetic movement to discourage the very people that Jesus came to save. He gave his life for the sick, the lost, those who have really messed up, the ones who people think have done the most wrong. In contrast, Jesus was upset with the ones who were so puffed up with pride that they thought they were always correct, full of their own rightness and winning at any cost (Luke 5:31–32). I've been there, and I'm not proud of those prideful days. I want to win—yes—but to gain true life, Jesus says I must lose my own self-centered life (Mark 8:35).

Basically, this wayward approach that is plaguing the Western church is to say that *what* is right and wrong is most important, but *how* we talk about right and wrong doesn't really matter. This overemphasis on the what reflects our current culture, and those who've grown up in the Western world have all been trained in it. It sounds like this: knowing *what* is right and wrong is way more important than *how* we communicate it. From schools, to standardized tests, to board exams and dissertations, the right information and answers are by far more vital to our culture than the process we use to get there. "Showing your work" on your assignments often seems to be more of a check to make sure you're not cheating than it is to evaluate correct methodology. Of course, exceptions exist, but generally speaking, the cultural value resides in the what, not the how. Having the correct information (what) seems to outweigh engaging the correct process (how) almost every time.

And here lies the problem for the Christian: such an overemphasis on the what is not the method Jesus modeled. If we really want to live from a biblical worldview, we must follow Jesus not just in *what* he said, but in *how* he said it. As we read through the four Gospels, we see Jesus strategically navigating discussions about the what depending on differing levels of relationship that he had with people. Jesus's brilliance about how to communicate led to different topics being discussed in corresponding contexts. Jesus demonstrated over and over that effective communication is not just *what* you say, but what is heard, and what someone hears is greatly affected by *how* you communicate it.

> *If we really want to live from a biblical worldview, we must follow Jesus not just in* what *he said, but in* how *he said it.*

Jesus is the Christian standard. As Christians, we must never become complacent to *how* Jesus modeled God's truth. We cannot ignore *how* he navigated social dilemmas. I believe we need to be equipped not just in *what* we know of God's Word but *how* we apply his Word. If we ignore the way Jesus communicated, we are throwing away a huge component of what made Jesus such an incredible teacher and leader. We would be dismissing a part of who he is because he is the way, the truth, and the life (John 24:6).

Now, John 24:6 might be a verse you've heard before, but let's pause for a moment and think about it more deeply. This verse means that truth is not just information, facts, or rules to follow. Truth is a person—Jesus. Truth is not a list of rights and wrongs to tell others about. Truth is a person to introduce others to. That massively changes things, doesn't it? That means that when I'm speaking truth to someone, I actually should be talking about a person who wants a relationship, not just to know what is right or wrong. The way Jesus embodied truth is both *what* and *how*. He emphasized this to his disciples as the main identifier of following him: "A new commandment I give to you, that you love one another: just as I have loved you, you also are to love one another. By this all people will know that you are my disciples, if you have love for one another" (John 13:34–35 ESV).

This is the harder path, the messier middle, and it will require us to depend on God in walking his way through social dilemmas.

> I know that even as I'm writing this, you or someone you may know could be thinking, See, there he goes. He's just going to avoid the hard issues—so weak. If you really believe something, you shout it as loud as you can! You make your best argument for that truth, and let the chips fall as they may—let the people fall as they may.

Here's the deal: I'm unwilling to prematurely let people "fall as they may." I love the church too much! I love my neighbors too much! I love people who are lost and broken too much. I know that at some point, people must make their own choices, and no one can do that for them. I get that, and it often breaks my heart. Choices are sacred because they set a direction that leads to a destination, and that destination has eternal consequences. No one knew this better than Jesus, and yet he was wholeheartedly committed to giving everyone the opportunity to choose him. He invited people into his love not just through *what* he said but *how* he said it, not just *what* he did but *how* he did it. That's all I'm trying to get at. Listen, *what* is right and wrong is still very important, but if we want to take obeying Jesus seriously, we also must follow *how* Jesus modeled right and wrong.

> *Choices are sacred because they set a direction that leads to a destination, and that destination has eternal consequences.*

This is the way of Jesus. So many of the people in Jesus's day who seemed to be trapped in sin the most absolutely loved hanging out with him. They didn't feel bullied by him or condemned by him. They didn't sense his wrath of retaliation as he contended for the faith. Not at all. They felt seen by him, heard by him, saved, and chosen by him. Their experience of Jesus was so much more than the *what*. It was the *how*. This is troubling because it seems vastly different than people's experience with Christians today. If Jesus is our model, we are to imitate him in every way.

In light of all of this, I want to be very clear. We're going to be journeying through how exactly to approach social dilemmas. This is a pertinent topic for all of us, and I believe God has much to say about it. We want and need to be equipped to enter every day into social dilemma conversations with a new ability to dialogue with our friends, classmates, roommates, coworkers, kids, girlfriend or boyfriend, and spouse about the way of Jesus.

Prayer

Lord, I know that there are already emotions and thoughts that are stirring in us as we approach this topic. We ask for your grace, your mercy, and your patience as we process your way. Please pour out your wisdom on us and meet us right where we are. We love you, and we trust you. In your name, Jesus, we pray, amen.

Social dilemmas seem to be around every corner, and they usually develop for one of two reasons. First, something is happening or being discussed, and we're not sure what to do or say. Should we engage, walk away, argue our viewpoint, or abandon ship? It could be something theological or about a relationship. It might be something about sexual immorality, pronouns, addictions, or politics. You don't want to hurt someone, but if you stay quiet, are you simply affirming what they believe, even though you don't believe it? It's a dilemma, and you feel stuck!

I've been there. This first type of social dilemma is probably the most common I've encountered in my own life. It can happen suddenly, but usually the situation grows in intensity and complexity over time until it reaches a breaking point.

When the second type of social dilemma occurs, it's often a surprise. Something is happening or being discussed, and we think we know what to do or say; in fact, we might be super-confident about it. So we respond, but afterward, we realize that it didn't go well at all. It certainly didn't go the way we were hoping. Now we're not sure what to do, because people didn't react the way we thought they would, and it's just caused another situation even more stressful and confusing than the first one. It's a dilemma, and you feel stuck!

I've been there too! So many times, I have wished I could take back how I responded in the moment. This has happened in person and online, and it doesn't feel great. These dilemmas that we have experienced and attempted to navigate often reveal that we are ill-equipped to engage those situations. We need help. We need a method that we can follow to make sure we are honoring God, regardless of the outcome. In order to discover that method, we must realize a common flaw in how we try to cross the traffic of most social dilemmas.

In those two types of social dilemmas, the focus is on *what* I should say or do without much emphasis on *how* I should say it or do it. Before we move any further, it's important to acknowledge that *how* we act or *what* we might say to people may change based on *who* we are talking to. For example, I was recently helping at our middle school summer camp. The students were going down a huge zipline over a small lake. You might be starting to sweat right now thinking about that; just hold on (pun completely intended). Now, from the platform high in the trees, this experience can be daunting. If I were talking to fearful students whom I had met only that week, I would focus on empathy first. Based on our dialogue, I would take either a reasoning route of the value that God has in facing our fears or an emotional route of encouragement focused on God's protection. However, if I was talking to one of my own kids, I would just quote one of our favorite movies—"Don't think; just do"—because we have years of relationship together. They know my heart, and that phrase is linked to all kinds of previous knowledge, experience, and awareness of God's protection. In these scenarios, the overall message I'm conveying would be similar, but how I would be communicating it would differ based on whom I was talking to.

How we say *what* we say differs based on the context of relationship we have with the individuals.

That's a good thing. That's contextualized conversation, and it's a skill we can develop to communicate most effectively in different scenarios. The difference in how we do this isn't based on one group being better than the other group, or being more truthful to one group over the other. It's simply what's most helpful based on what we know about each other and the current state of our relationship. This sort of adjustment allows for more effective communication. In fact, this is where so much great research has been done in emotional intelligence. Jesus was great at this. He knew that the most loving expression of truth comes from intentional contextualization. Context is key!

The idea of contextualization can be a slippery slope based on how we sort different contexts. Unfortunately, we often employ various ways of categorizing that can lead to racial profiling, stereotyping, and other judgmental generalizations. That's not what we're going after here. How we differentiate people really matters. Our highest priority is not about making sure that we don't hurt someone's feelings, though that's important. Our highest priority is being intentional about the contextualized details of how Jesus differentiated people. Following the model and method of Jesus is always most important.

Let's look at a social dilemma that Jesus had and see what he established.

> While Jesus was still talking to the crowd, his mother and brothers stood outside, wanting to speak to him. Someone told him, "Your mother and brothers are standing outside, wanting to speak to you." He replied to him, "Who is my mother, and who are my brothers?" Pointing to his disciples, he said, "Here are my mother and my brothers. For whoever does the will of my Father in heaven is my brother and sister and mother." (Matt. 12:46–50 NIV)

Can you imagine the reaction of Mary and Jesus's brothers to Jesus's response? I would say "shocked" might be an understatement.

In this situation, we see Jesus creating an important distinction: family versus non-family. He established an important context that would determine how he communicated. He defined family as "whoever does the will of my Father in heaven" or "those who hear the word of God and do it" (Luke 8:21). He defined everyone else as non-family, even if they were biological family. I realize in our day and age, this may seem a bit harsh, as if Jesus was being rude to his biological family; however, this was part of his perfect method

of navigating social dilemmas. He wanted to be clear about his contextualization between family and non-family. We have no indica-
tion in scripture that this categorization as non-family resulted in
Jesus withdrawing any of his love from his biological family. This
differentiation does not change the amount of love that is expressed,
only *how* it may be expressed. With those that Jesus had a lifelong
relationship with, the most loving thing he could do was to be simple and clear with how his contextualization was going to work.
Only those who were following Jesus, doing the will of the heavenly
Father, were in his "family." Let's call everyone else "guests" because
they weren't in the family yet (according to Jesus's definition), but
they're still invited. They are to be loved and treated with honor and
respect. In this one scene, Jesus set the trajectory for all the other
social dilemmas he encountered. The *how* of communicating in a
social dilemma is based on *who* is involved in it. In other words, we
can expect that *how* Jesus communicated his truth to those in the
family would be different than with guests.

We see Jesus explain this more near the end of one of his sermons.

> Why do you look at the speck of sawdust in your brother's eye
> and pay no attention to the plank in your own eye? How can
> you say to your brother, "Let me take the speck out of your
> eye," when all the time there is a plank in your own eye? You
> hypocrite, first take the plank out of your own eye, and then
> you will see clearly to remove the speck from your brother's
> eye. "Do not give dogs what is sacred; do not throw your pearls
> to pigs. If you do, they may trample them under their feet, and
> turn and tear you to pieces." (Matt. 7:3–6 NIV)

Jesus was talking to those claiming to be in the family. He was
helping them to be aware of their hypocrisy and to do something
about their own sin before focusing on someone else's. This is part of

the will of God the Father that they were supposedly trying to follow. We see Jesus challenging those in the family directly and then empowering them on what they should do. Notice that he didn't prevent them from holding another family member accountable. Jesus was saying that those who are grieved and humbled by their own sin are better able to engage in family accountability conversations. In contrast, guests are not able to receive truth in this way. In fact, Jesus said that if the family tries to communicate right and wrong or accountability in the same way to the guests, they will not only reject it, but they may become angry and turn to attack the family. For the sake of clarity, Jesus used words that Jewish culture would have connected with the Gentiles (i.e., "dogs" and "pigs"). Jesus was not talking about hating them, withdrawing love from them, or judging them in some way. Instead, he was helping the family to recognize that *how* they should communicate in a social dilemma is based on *who* is involved in it. He certainly wanted to communicate truth in love to the guests, but it must be a different way than how the family talks to each other.

Let's bring this directly into our own lives. In Jesus's example, we can see a difference in how we should be communicating and interacting with those who follow Jesus and those who don't. It doesn't make one group better than the other; it is simply how God's love is expressed most effectively. There are two different missions God is highlighting here: For the family, Jesus wants to move them deeper and further into relationship with God. This is sanctification. For the guests, Jesus's love comes alongside to provide for them and save them from the massive consequences of sin in this life and forever. This is justification. Jesus is incredibly strategic. Jesus wants to meet people right where they are, but he loves them too much to leave them there. For the family, he is always encouraging more steps of refinement, and for the guests, he wants to invite them into the family. For Jesus, the goal of every social dilemma is greater relationship, so based on the context, he's going to do the next step that each relationship requires.

> *Jesus wants to meet people right where they are, but he loves them too much to leave them there.*

As we look at another specific social dilemma, let's pay attention to how Jesus interacted differently with family than with guests.

> Then Jesus went around teaching from village to village. Calling the Twelve to him, he began to send them out two by two and gave them authority over impure spirits. These were his instructions: "Take nothing for the journey except a staff—no bread, no bag, no money in your belts. Wear sandals but not an extra shirt. Whenever you enter a house, stay there until you leave that town. And if any place will not welcome you or listen to you, leave that place and shake the dust off your feet as a testimony against them." They went out and preached that people should repent. They drove out many demons and anointed many sick people with oil and healed them. (Mark 6:7–13 NIV)

This had to be an unreal adventure for the disciples. Can you imagine? Healings and casting out demons, while at the same time dealing with disbelief in people. What a mixture of emotions!

Interestingly, there was no calling down fire from heaven if the villagers (guests) didn't believe. The disciples were simply to respect what the villagers had decided, and move on. *What about righteous anger? What about contending for the faith?* I'm sure the disciples were frustrated, angry, and confused at times, but they knew their thoughts and feelings should never override their obedience to God.

Jesus had been very clear about his method. What's also fascinating is that the disciples were only asked to provide a testimony of the villagers' decision, to *shake the dust off their feet*. Jesus did not command them to judge the village by creating a sentence, enacting punishment, or developing a process of correction or discipline. Clearly, they were to leave those actions up to God (see the account in Matt. 10:15 for God's eventual judgment).

The method of Jesus in social dilemmas is starting to become clear. He was going to challenge and empower his family. In the previous scenario, Jesus did this by asking his disciples to take almost nothing on their journey, and they would be empowered by the Holy Spirit. For guests, Jesus would provide what they needed physically and spiritually while also respecting their faith decisions. Going village to village, the disciples were to share the gospel message, heal the sick, and cast out demons, and they also were to leave the village if faith in Christ was not welcomed.

FOR FAMILY: *Challenge and empower*
FOR GUESTS: *Provide and respect*

The disciples came back from their adventure, and they began sharing with Jesus what had happened, when suddenly the news of John the Baptist's beheading reached Jesus. Wow, talk about parallel tracks. Sometimes something amazing is happening simultaneously with something tragic. This had to be heart-wrenching news, and so we see in the scriptures that Jesus went off to pray, which is something that he did often (see also Luke 5:16): "When Jesus heard what had happened, he withdrew by boat privately to a solitary place" (Matt. 14:13–21).

I obviously don't know exactly what Jesus was praying about, but I can imagine that discerning his Father's will was a part of it,

father's will to not help John

considering that he never did anything without seeing the Father do it (John 5:19). Just imagine the options that Jesus had. Would he take down Rome for killing his cousin? He could have done this individually, with a host of angels, or through rallying up a crowd of Jewish people. He had the option of making a public display of how wrong the government was with thorough arguments and evidence. He could have immediately judged all the people who were on Rome's side from those who weren't and then start enacting accountability, justice, or punitive measures. He could have demanded an audience with Herod to voice his thoughts and opinions on what he felt was right and wrong. Any and all of these options are things that we might do, given a similar scenario, but not Jesus.

Instead of all these options for navigating this profoundly personal social dilemma, he chose to deepen his connection with his heavenly Father. The priority for Jesus in this social dilemma was his relationship with God the Father. Relationship is always the goal in every social dilemma—relationship with God and relationship with others, with prayer being a vital component.

With this recognition of the critical nature of prayer, the Jesus Method is further taking shape.

THE **JESUS** METHOD

STEP 1 Prayer

STEP 2A If family, then challenge and empower

STEP 2B If guests, then provide and respect

Let's continue where we left off in this social dilemma to see how this method of Jesus was applied to his family (his disciples) and the guests (the crowd).

> When Jesus heard what had happened, he withdrew by boat privately to a solitary place. **[Step 1]** Hearing of this, the crowds followed him on foot from the towns. When Jesus landed and saw a large crowd, he had compassion on them and healed their sick. **[Step 2b—provide for their needs]** As evening approached, the disciples came to him and said, "This is a remote place, and it's already getting late. Send the crowds away, so they can go to the villages and buy themselves some food." Jesus replied, "They do not need to go away. You give them something to eat."
>
> "We have here only five loaves of bread and two fish," they answered. "Bring them here to me," he said. And he directed the people to sit down on the grass. Taking the five loaves and the two fish and looking up to heaven, he gave thanks and broke the loaves. Then he gave them to the disciples, and the disciples gave them to the people. **[Step 2a—empower]** They all ate and were satisfied, **[Step 2b—provide]** and the disciples picked up twelve basketfuls of broken pieces that were left over. The number of those who ate was about five thousand men, besides women and children. Immediately Jesus made the disciples get into the boat and go on ahead of him to the other side, **[Step 2a—challenge]** while he dismissed the crowd. **[Step 2b—respect]** After he had dismissed them, he went up on a mountainside by himself to pray. **[Step 1—prayer]** Later that night, he was there alone . . . (Matt. 14:13–21)

We see plenty in this account that we could unpack, but for the sake of this discussion on social dilemmas, it's important to understand the composition of the crowd. This happened in a Jewish region as indicated not only by the physical location, but also by the numerical symbolism: five loaves like the five books of the Torah and twelve baskets relating to the twelve tribes of Israel. It is reasonable, then, to assume that this was a Jewish crowd. Notice, however, that Jesus only treated his disciples as family, challenging and empowering them. He provided for and respected the crowd as guests. Once again, he clarified his contextualization, just as he did with his biological family. He continued to refine his meaning of family as a category not gained from biology or from culture.

Family was not determined by the sum of the crowd's right and wrong behavior or how often they went to synagogue. Family was defined by doing the will of the heavenly Father. For us, then, family is not determined by growing up in the church, attendance, donation records, volunteer hours, list of good deeds, or any number of the other statistics we might come up with. It is the same definition today as it was when Jesus first formed it: those following Jesus, doing the will of the heavenly Father. Though this seems very clear, I offer a caution on a common mistake. We can often assume someone is in the family because of all those aforementioned behaviors, when we really don't know. Jesus didn't make that assumption. He demonstrated in the feeding of the 5,000 that he categorized people as guests until he had clarity about their willingness to be in the family. With this in mind, let's add another detail to the method that we see modeled by Jesus:

THE **JESUS** METHOD

STEP 1   Prayer

STEP 2A If family, then challenge and empower

STEP 2B If guest, then provide and respect

**If unsure whether they are family or guest, treat them as a guest.

I think it's helpful to pause at the end of each chapter and take time to meditate on the material. I'm aware this might not be something you're used to. I also realize that if your goal is to read this book as fast as possible, this method is going to slow you down. I think that's a good thing. I believe that inviting God into a time of prayerful reflection on what we just covered can unlock new insights and equip us more fully. Enjoy some hang-out time with God.

Prayerful Reflection

1. What is a new insight?
2. Is there anybody in my life whom I have put in the wrong category?
3. What is challenging to you about this material?
4. What questions do you have?
5. What specific relationship does God want you to be praying for?

CHAPTER 2

IT'S ALL ABOUT RELATIONSHIP

One of my all-time favorite movie moments is from a movie that we used to watch with our kids. Well, they would be watching it in the car, and I would only be listening to it, which means I practically have it memorized at this point! In the movie, the main character was faced with a decision to either stand up and fight for what he believed in or give in to the enemy's demands. At that moment, he started to sing a song, "No, I won't back down . . . I'm gonna stand my ground." The emotion and resolve is so strong! You can feel the decisiveness in his spirit to fight for what he believes in. I can resonate with that. I can get pretty fired up! When we think about social dilemmas, we often experience a similar heated reaction: "I'm *not* backing down!" *it is my Personality*

I don't like backing down to anything. Backing down to me seems like losing, and I don't like to lose! I prefer the story of the teenager shepherd boy David, who stood up to the giant Goliath. Goliath was causing a big social dilemma for the Israelites, and David didn't back down. He took that big boy down! When everyone else was scared and backing down, too weak and afraid, David

sometimes it is not only the right thing to do, But imparative

didn't just stand up for what he believed in, he took the fight to the enemy. It's like he said, "No, I won't back down . . . I'm gonna stand my ground." As inspiring as this story and many others like it are, we need to recognize a danger. Stories like these throughout the Bible can lead Christians to assume that not backing down should always be the answer to social dilemmas.

No Never + always

I don't like backing down to anything.

I know that we all can have this same sort of reaction to the pressurized predicaments going on in our world right now. We may feel threatened and have a desire to stand up and fight. However, we learned in chapter 1 that refusing to back down, as a blanket method of reaction to everything and everyone, isn't what Jesus modeled. I'll admit it: I kind of wish it was, but it's not. This is hard for me to digest, and I assume it is for many of us. If it's any consolation, it was difficult for Jesus's disciples too. Even after being with Jesus for three years, Peter drew his sword and was ready to not back down when Jesus was arrested in the garden of Gethsemane. As we see Jesus rebuke Peter, we realize that the way of Jesus is not just countercultural; it's beyond the natural way we want to react. Out of our love, respect, and honor for Jesus, we want to stand up for him, not back down when people are attacking the truth. I get it, which is why we need to continue to seek God in this journey of discerning the Jesus Method in social dilemmas. I think it's a good time to pray.

Prayer

Lord, we don't want to be weak, and we don't want to have misguided strength. Please help us to humbly come before you now, willing and wanting to learn more about your way. If there is any anger or unfor-giveness that we have in our hearts for people who oppose you, Lord, reveal that to us so that we can hand those people over to you. It is not our place to judge, regardless of how we feel or how much we want to. Lord, fill us with the fruit of your Spirit right now as we take a moment to connect with you in relationship. In Jesus's name we pray, amen.

As a metacognitive exercise, let's review. In social dilemmas, our culture has often taught us that *what* is right and wrong is the most important, and *how* we go about communicating that is sec-ondary at best. In addition, contemporary culture posits that if we really believe in something, we should shout about it passionately as often as we possibly can wherever we are. That's *how* we should do it. Current culture, however, does allow for a quieter alterna-tive, but it's no less wrong. Namely, if we want to be more loving, we should not say anything at all. We should have self-control and be silent. Even though you may know what's right, keep it to yourself so you don't hurt anyone's feelings. Unfortunately, *how* we communicate God's truth has been relegated in our society to either some sort of righteous anger or reluctant silence. Neither of these reflects Jesus's method.

We see a different way of communicating as we look at the Jesus Method. Jesus strategically navigated discussions about *what* is right and wrong based on the context of relationship that he had with people. Often, it was *how* Jesus communicated right and wrong that really separated his way from the ways of the world. As a result, fol-lowers of Jesus must pay attention to how Jesus modeled interacting with those who say they follow Jesus (family) versus those who don't (guests). Contextualization of communication doesn't make one group better than the other. It's simply how God's love is expressed most accurately.

This is where we are so far:

THE **JESUS** METHOD

STEP 1   Prayer

STEP 2A   If family, then challenge and empower

STEP 2B   If guest, then provide and respect

**If unsure whether they are family or guest, treat them as a guest.

We already discussed how Peter struggled with the don't-back-down mentality the night that Jesus was betrayed. Now, let's listen to an older, wiser Peter as he reflects on the cross of Christ as an extremely violent and volatile social dilemma that Jesus endured.

Suffer for Him?

> To this you were called, because Christ suffered for you, leaving you an example, that you should follow in his steps. "He committed no sin, and no deceit was found in his mouth." When they hurled their insults at him, he did not retaliate; when he suffered, he made no threats. Instead, he entrusted himself to him who judges justly. (1 Pet. 2:21–23 NIV)

But I am not Jesus & here for the

Fully God and fully human, after thirty-plus years of training in the will of his Heavenly Father, Jesus navigated a brutal, unjust, misinformed social dilemma with no retaliation—none! Jesus didn't even have a muttered threat under his breath. Why did he do it that way? He knew that retaliation was not the goal. His goal was relationship, and **retaliation does not play a role in strengthening relationships**. Instead, he leaned into his relationship with his heavenly Father, completely trusting in *him who judges justly*. Perfect

Purpose to die for the sins of the world. Can't do it

Jesus, who was fully capable of judging others, and the only one justified to do so, surrendered his right to judge. He forfeited this right
so that everyone could have the opportunity for right relationship
with God.

The question we need to ask ourselves is, *Did Jesus back down?*
Did he back down according to the world's perspective? Yes, because
the world is focused on temporal victories of power, position, and the
pride of being right. What about from God's perspective? No. Jesus
didn't back down. Actually, he was standing up for eternal relationships. The goal of God is relationship. In any social dilemma, if
our goal is outside of Christ-modeled relationship, we're outside the
goal of God. This is a very dangerous place to be because we won't
find Jesus leading us there, and I don't ever want to go where Jesus
isn't leading.

*In any social dilemma, if our goal is outside of Christ-modeled
relationship, we're outside the goal of God.*

Think. Family

Let's go back to that night in the garden of Gethsemane when
Jesus was betrayed by Judas. Jesus was face to face with guests coming to arrest him. All of those guests had already either been provided the truth directly or indirectly over the last three years. They
had all made their decisions on who they were going to follow, and
it wasn't Jesus. So, in surrendering to his arrest, Jesus fulfilled his
method, respecting where the soldiers were on their faith journey
and trusting himself to his heavenly Father. Jesus was consistent
in fulfilling his method, regardless of the circumstances that each
social dilemma brought, even if they were life-threatening.

Comparing the Jesus Method with what I routinely see in current Christian culture, I've concluded that when we do not know
the way of Jesus, we weaponize the truth of Jesus. Let that sink in

for a second. I know it's a strong statement. Communicating *what* Jesus said without *how* he said it assimilates us into the ways of the world. The result is that we start using our beliefs as a means to prove we are right, win an argument, get what we want, or put someone in their place. All those goals lie outside the goal of God. I have never seen this overemphasis on *what* is right and wrong grow relationship with guests, but I have seen it break relationships with guests and tear apart the family itself many times. It's not the method of Jesus.

> *When we do not know the way of Jesus, we weaponize the truth of Jesus.*

what dilemma's

As we are starting to understand how Jesus entered these dilemmas, I want to step back and ask an important question: In all of these types of dilemmas, why would we choose to engage them at all? It clearly takes our limited resources of time, energy, attention, and money (TEAM). These four areas of our life are ways in which we can grow or diminish relationships, and we only have so much of them. **Wherever our TEAM goes, relationship grows**. A common response could be, "Why would I spend it on these sorts of dilemmas? They can be so exhausting! It doesn't even seem worth it. What's to be accomplished in entering into any of this? What's the goal? I already have enough conflict in my own life, so why would I want to be in more of it? I don't feel like it, and it's not like I'm going to make a difference anyway. It's better to turn it all off and avoid it all. I'll do my own thing."

There's a problem, however, with this type of response from Christians. Taking even a cursory look at Jesus's ministry and his commissioning of his followers to go into all the world and make disciples (Matt. 28:19–20), conflict seems inevitable. Disagreements and social dilemmas are *going* to happen. It's not a matter of *if* they happen, only *when* they happen. We see social dilemmas all through the book of Acts even within the family itself. If we're trying to follow Jesus's worldwide commissioning, there will be social dilemmas to engage.

We know that conflict and disagreement often lead to disunity. More than just a disruption of relationship, many times it becomes a division. As a pastor, this is what I often hear from people leaving the church or people who would never want to be a part of a church: "I don't want to be a part of unresolved conflict and disagreements that are causing disunity and division." They see all the fighting that is happening within the global church and Christian culture, and they've had enough or they have no desire to be a part of any of that.

I get it! Man, do I get it! The effects surrounding social dilemmas being mishandled can cause tremendous destruction within the family and with guests. It's why we must be equipped to handle these agreements and disagreements better, using the Jesus Method.

People today assume disagreement is synonymous with disunity, as well as the opposite, that agreement equals unity. This is what it can sound like: "Unity assumes uniformity (being the same); unity means you agree with me on everything. You can't be with me if you disagree with me. You can't be for me and you can't love me if you don't agree with me on everything." In the past, unity meant there was something stronger that holds us together, despite our differences of opinion or disagreements. I don't get that sense anymore. This trend toward disunity if we disagree really concerns me, and I'm not alone. It really concerned Jesus too.

A few hours before Jesus was betrayed and arrested, the disciples were celebrating the Passover meal in the Upper Room. As they were leaving, they were walking and talking, crossing the Kidron Valley, and Jesus began to pray. Let's think for a second about his mental and emotional state only hours before being handed over to the worst torture that humans could imagine. Whatever he was praying about must have been of utmost concern to him. After three years, now he only had a little bit of time left, and he was pleading to God the Father about what was heaviest on his heart. Let's listen in:

> My prayer is not for them alone. I pray also for those who will believe in me through their message, that all of them may be one, Father, just as you are in me and I am in you. May they also be in us so that the world may believe that you have sent me. I have given them the glory that you gave me, that they may be one as we are one—I in them and you in me—so that they may be brought to complete unity. Then the world will know that you sent me and have loved them even as you have loved me. (John 17:20–22 NIV)

It's incredible that Jesus's greatest concern for his family in that moment was not something about beliefs or doctrine, but about division and disunity. The potential disruption in the relationship that we have with God and with each other was weighing heavily on his heart. Why? Because unity is for the purpose of the world (guests) believing in him. Despite all the ways the world will try to divide his followers and rip the Church apart, it's unity in Jesus's family that will be the greatest evidence, the best witness, that Jesus is who he said he is. Our unified relationship with God is what is intended to unify our relationships with each other. This is why the goal of God is relationship.

Jesus is our example, and so his goal becomes the family's goal. Yes, God's goal of relationship is for the family, and it's for rest of the world too: "For God so loved the world that he gave his one and only Son, that whoever believes in him shall not perish but have eternal life. For God did not send his Son into the world to condemn the world, but to save the world through him" (John 3:16–17 NIV).

Relationship has always been the goal. God wants further relationship with his family and restored relationship with guests. No matter what we have done or failed to do, the goal is always a growing relationship with God and with others. The family must understand how much God loves his family and the guests too. Yes, he loves us *and* them. God's love is not limited; it never runs out.

Let's take this goal of God and move it into the topic of disagreement and social dilemmas. What should be our goal when we enter into conflict or disagreement? Relationship! Here's the question I ask myself sometimes when I'm in the middle of a social dilemma conversation: "Am I seeking relationship [God's goal] or just being right [the world's goal]?" I can have a priority of being right or a priority of relationship, but not both. One of them must be first. What did Jesus choose? Going back to John 3:17, Jesus came to save the world, not condemn it. That sounds like relationship is Jesus's first priority. How about for you and me? We must be honest with ourselves. Oh, this is so much easier said than done, but it's clear what God expects from his family. It's OK if you feel convicted right now; I know I do!

> I can have a priority of being right or a priority of relationship, but not both.

When we read scripture, we need to be humble enough to let it read us back. Conviction is not a push down, it's a hand up. Condemnation pushes us down, making us believe that what we did equals who we are. It sounds like, "We made a mistake, therefore we are a mistake." That's not from God. That's the enemy talking to you. Conviction is a helping hand up. It's God's way of inviting us into a better way with him. Conviction is like rumble strips on the side of the road. Rumble strips are not comfortable or quiet to go over, and they usually wake everyone up in the car. Their purpose is inviting you back onto the road, where you're meant to be. It's the same with conviction. The Holy Spirit is inviting you back into the way of God, where you're meant to be. Of course, you can ignore God's invitation, just like you can ignore those rumble strips on the road, but there will be consequences if you do. That's not a threat; it's called reality.

Valuing relationships over valuing being right cannot only be a theoretical decision. It should be a wrestling in our hearts. At the end of the day, we must ask ourselves how badly we just want to be right versus how badly we want relationship. Only you and God know the answer to that one. Ask God about it right now. God might want to tell you where your heart is, so keep track of whatever God is revealing. What we say is the overflow of our hearts (Luke 6:45b NIV), and everything we do flows from it (Prov. 4:23), so don't miss what God is trying to expose about your heart. Remember, it's conviction, not condemnation. It might feel like rumble strips because he's trying to invite you back on the road he has for you.

We have finally arrived at the root of every social dilemma. Are you ready for the big reveal? At the root of every social dilemma is a heart dilemma. What do we really want? Do we really want what God wants? Do we really want further relationship—not *how I want* relationship or *how someone else wants* relationship, but how God models relationship. His model is all grace and all truth all the time. Is it challenging and empowering the family in a loving way and providing for the needs of guests while respecting where they are in faith?

At the root of every social dilemma is a heart dilemma.

I want to say it again before we move on: at the root of every social dilemma is a heart dilemma. What do we really want? The answer to that question will either align us with God's will or take us away from it. It's that important! If we are about to post something online, respond to that email (you know the one), or say something face to face with someone and our heart is not aligned with God's goal, we should pause and pray. We can always go back to step 1 of the Jesus Method. It's the foundation. By praying, you're not wasting an opportunity or being weak; you are following the way of Jesus, growing relationship with the heavenly Father. As you pray, with humility and a desire to know the Father's will, God will continue to put on your heart how to move forward.

Jesus did this sort of "pause and pray" all the time. One of my favorites is when Jesus prayed all night before he chose his twelve apostles (Luke 6:12). These were the guys that he would be growing in relationship with and trusting to go out into all the world and make disciples. It's a big-time decision that would involve many social dilemmas. He didn't rush it, he spent time in prayer, and his heart became aligned with the goal of relationship, ready to do the Father's will. Jesus was deeply committed to step 1 of his method. It's not a last resort, it's the first step, and we can return to it any time during a social dilemma.

In one of the most heart-wrenching stories in the Bible for me, we see Jesus stay committed to relationship, even as a heart dilemma was playing out right in front of him: "As He was setting out on a journey, a man ran up to Him and knelt before Him, and asked Him, 'Good Teacher, what shall I do so that I may inherit eternal life?'" (Mark 10:17 NASB).

First of all, men running in biblical times was not usual, especially those in power. This man's pursuit of Jesus clearly was earnest. Since he asked, "What shall I do?," we know that the man thought eternal life is something to be gained or achieved. He thought that moral behavior is the ultimate goal and a requirement of God. Even though he clearly was a ruler of some sort with control, power, and money, by asking this question, he seemed to feel insecure about his situation. Can we relate to this dilemma? Perhaps we aren't rulers in the sense that this man was, but his temptation to believe that moral behavior is the ultimate goal is very common. Surprisingly, no one had asked a question of this magnitude of Jesus yet, not even his own disciples. This is the most essential question that anyone could ask. There are no higher stakes than all of eternity! "But Jesus said to him, 'Why do you call me good? No one is good except God alone'" (Mark 10:18).

One of the attributes that we see in Jesus's method in social dilemmas is that he rarely simply answered someone's question. He always realized that there is a questioner behind the question. A questioner with whom he wants relationship. Remember, that was always his goal. Most of the time this led Jesus to enter dialogue and conversation. Jesus responded to the man's question with a question. Classic Jesus! Jesus challenged the man's faulty assumption that "goodness" is determined by one's achievement. Only God was "good" in Jewish culture, and so, if Jesus would have agreed with the man, he could have been perceived by others as blasphemous: "You know the commandments: 'Do not murder, Do not commit adultery, Do not steal, Do not give false testimony, Do not defraud, Honor your father and mother.' And he said to Him, 'Teacher, I have kept all these things from my youth'" (Mark 10:19–20).

I love how the man picked up on Jesus's teaching. He dropped the "good" when addressing him. This is a smart guy. He really wanted to know the answer to his question, or at least he thought he did. He was so focused on what is right and wrong that he missed the whole point of faith: a relationship with God. He stated that he had done all the right things, and Jesus—wait for it—did not disagree with him on this. Surely this man had messed up. He had to have done wrong things, but Jesus refused to turn this social dilemma into a faultfinding discussion on right and wrong. Jesus had a higher priority that he wanted to spend his time on: relationship. How often are we distracted from the main goal of God by nitpicking the sins of someone else or even their opinions on a topic? Even if those things occur, Jesus demonstrated that we must stay locked in on trying to build right relationship: "Looking at him, Jesus showed love to him and said to him, 'One thing you lack: go and sell all you possess and give to the poor, and you will have treasure in heaven; and come, follow Me'" (Mark 10:21).

It's important that we don't fly over this verse too quickly. Exegeting the original language reveals that this "looking at him" at the beginning of the verse is an intensified version of the verb. Jesus was looking intently, eye to eye, assessing or examining the man's heart. There must have been something admirable in the man because this is the only place in the entire Gospel of Mark that it says Jesus "showed love" (ESV) to someone like this. This is the agape form of love, the unconditional, sacrificial love of God. It doesn't get any better than this! We can tell from the language used that Jesus was not looking at a hypocrite, trying to pull one over on Jesus. This is important to understand because not every social dilemma we face is going to be with malicious people who want to embarrass us. Sometimes our social dilemmas are with people who are well-intended and mean no harm.

Jesus had before him a man who claimed to be a part of the family, so Jesus was going to challenge him and give him the key to be empowered by God now and forever. The man had replaced his relationship with God with a relationship with riches, breaking the first commandment. The choice of who or what to worship was hanging in the balance for this man: relationship with God or relationship with the world. Choices are sacred because they set a direction that leads to a destination. Even though the man seemed to have done everything right in his own eyes, he still had a problem. His heart was torn in a dilemma. "But he was deeply dismayed by these words, and he went away grieving; for he was one who owned much property" (Mark 10:22).

> *Choices are sacred because they set a direction that leads to a destination.*

He didn't really want what God had to offer. With the way, truth, and life standing right in front of him, he walked away. This is heart-wrenching for me and very sobering at the same time. Jesus let people walk away when they didn't want the relationship he had to offer. Get this: Jesus even let kind, well-intentioned, morally sound people walk away from him if they didn't want relationship with him. Relationship is the goal.

Unfortunately, like this young ruler, I wonder how many times I've walked away from Jesus when my heart wanted something other than more relationship with God. When I do this, I'm usually upset and ask, "Where did you go, God?" Of course, he's not the one who moved. God's heart has always wanted relationship with me, but my heart gets so distracted sometimes! I might still be very kind, following all the rules with top-level morality, but my heart is walking away from Jesus.

We see again in this tragedy that right and wrong behavior always needs to take a back seat to relationship with Jesus. Our desire to grow in relationship with Jesus by listening and obeying him must be primary. As I was meditating on this passage, I had a convicting thought. Even if we get all the right and wrong beliefs and behavior correct, we could still be missing what is most important: relationship. If our goal in social dilemmas is simply to correct behavior or ensure right or wrong beliefs in our friends, kids, politicians, coworkers, and family, the best we could ever do is produce a bunch of rich, young rulers. Individuals who think they've done everything they need to do, but are actually lacking the very thing they truly need: a heart that wants relationship with God. To be transparent, I'm afraid this may be the harvest that many churches have a tendency to grow—people who may be nice, have good morals, follow the rules, do a lot of good things for people, and know a lot about God but still don't know him personally. According to Jesus, that's not good enough. Relationship is the goal of God, nothing less. People must want it in order to get it. It's a choice that only they can make.

Even if we get all the right and wrong beliefs and behavior correct, we could still be missing what is most important: relationship.

Jesus was saying to this man that his relationship with money was keeping him from a relationship with God. The man thought being right would save him, but it's only an unrivaled relationship with Christ that does that. His heart was in a dilemma that was causing a social dilemma. Jesus was providing for this man the very thing that he needed: the way to full life. He had to get rid of anything that blocked relationship with God. Then he could follow Jesus.

The man's heart made its choice, and it wasn't Jesus.

Though the young ruler had made the wrong choice, Jesus respected it. Think about that. Jesus did not chase him down to argue the validity of his point or try to convince or persuade the man that Jesus was right and the man was wrong. Jesus knew that you can't correct someone into relationship. Jesus did not retaliate in any way, strike him down, punish, shame, make fun of, or condemn him. Jesus let him walk away. By letting him go, Jesus was also being clear about something else. God was unwilling to accept, tolerate, agree to, or accommodate a lower level of relationship simply because that's what the man wanted. Jesus values real relationship too much to ever cheapen it. Relationship is not on the terms of the person you are in a dilemma with. It's on God's terms. This is an important point for those of us who are in social dilemmas with people who demand we agree with them. Such people may threaten that our love of them rides on our agreement with them. However, that is not what we see demonstrated by Jesus with the rich, young ruler. Jesus loved him deeply, but he did not agree with the man's heart posture. As the man walked away, Jesus's love for him did not diminish. The rich ruler had decided to not accept it.

Throughout this interaction with the rich, young ruler, Jesus engaged his method in a comprehensive manner. The man claimed to be family, so Jesus challenged and empowered him with a next step of relationship with God. As soon as the man was identified as a guest, Jesus, who had already provided the way to right relationship with God, respected the man's choice and let him leave. He knew that every social dilemma is rooted in the heart. The point of this encounter isn't just about money stealing our hearts. It's about the vulnerability that we all have for our hearts to be stolen or distracted by any number of things. Humanity is creative in all the ways we can break relationship with God, including focusing too much on what is right and wrong. In fact, there was once a story about a couple who got fatally distracted by their desire to focus on the knowledge of good and evil instead of relationship with God, and it didn't turn out well for them. Adam and Eve demonstrated at the beginning of God's story that humanity is incredibly vulnerable to an overemphasis on knowing *what* is right and wrong.

You can have your love of riches or Jesus, but not both. You can focus on being right or have a relationship with Jesus, but not both. We can talk all day about right and wrong and whether we have followed God's rules and regulations, or we can grow a relationship of reliance on God, but not both. That choice is sacred with eternal consequences of heaven or hell, and Jesus will respect whatever decision we make.

Can you imagine the self-control of Jesus to let the man go? Jesus respected the man's decision to not want God and the full life Jesus had for him now and forever. Jesus loved him truly, and true love requires choice. True love must be voluntary. It's why choices are so sacred.

Since relationship is God's goal, it's important to take a moment to talk about different levels of relationship. Not all relationships are created equal, and God wants the best relationship possible. To understand these different levels, we first need to talk about how we can grow relationships. I've already shared about TEAM (time, energy, attention, money). Wherever your TEAM goes, relationship grows. These are four dials you can turn up or down to increase or decrease relationship. When you start to give your TEAM, your heart is drawn more to that thing or person in which you're investing.

Relationships don't have to be only with people. We are more than capable of building relationships with pretty much anything. For example, if I spend a great deal of my TEAM on my phone, there's a relationship there. I can miss it when it's gone, be mad at it when it's not working right, feel angry when I can't find it, dread what I might find on it, and be happy when I'm playing music or games on it. That certainly sounds like relationship!

When it comes to TEAM, it's not always about the *quantity* of these elements. Often it can be the *quality* of them that matters most. For example, what's the first thing I do with my time each day? Where do I spend my best energy, or what are my best attention spans of my day? You get the idea. It's what Jesus talked about when he said, "Where someone's treasure is their heart is there also" (Matt. 6:21). If you want to grow a relationship, literally any relationship, just give more TEAM to it, your best TEAM to it, and watch what happens. At the same time, if you ever wonder where your heart is and why it may seem far from God or loved ones, look back over the last few months and track your TEAM. It's there that you'll find your heart. You might not like the picture your TEAM paints, but it is a reality that you can face and start to change.

That's how we grow relationship, and since that's God's goal, we can pretty much expect that God is going to challenge or test the family in each of these areas in our life. All our heart dilemmas are based on what we want to do with our TEAM. God wants our heart, and so God will give us plenty of opportunities to contribute our TEAM to him.

If those last few paragraphs are hitting you like a brick right now, it's OK. I remember the first time I was thinking through the TEAM concept. I was astounded by how true it was in my marriage, family, friendships, and workplace. I could trace back over my entire life and see how God tested each element of my TEAM. Over and over God gave me opportunities to trust in him more, depend on him more, and let him be in control. I passed some of those tests and failed others for sure. But he kept pursuing me. If that's where you are at right now, it's OK. Just put the book down and go and pray. Ask God some more questions about what he's trying to tell you concerning your TEAM. Ask him what relationships you're forming, weakening, or strengthening right now because of how you're allocating your TEAM. Regardless of what you think you're doing or what you're hoping for, God will help you see reality. Talk to God. God is for you, and this might be a moment for you to gain better perspective in your relationships.

> *Regardless of what you think you're doing or what you're hoping for, God will help you see reality.*

Now that we understand how relationships grow, let's talk about the different levels of them that we experience in life.

LEVEL 1

Getting Something—Selfishness

This is where you are simply getting something from someone or something else. It's a relationship that is full of yourself—what you want, when you want it, and how you want it. Technically, it's still a relationship because there is TEAM involved with another entity, but it's all for your benefit.

LEVEL 2

Giving and Getting Something—Self-protection

In the second level, you're giving some of your TEAM to another person or thing, but you're controlling the risk. A wide range of TEAM can exist in this level, from giving more than you get to getting more than you give. The key is that you're still protecting yourself. You're always getting at least something out of this level of relationship.

Giving without Getting Something—Selflessness

This level of relationship requires a high level of TEAM. It's a relationship in which you give and don't get anything in return. This has potential for tremendous depth. You're truly thinking about yourself less, which brings good relational potential. However, it's not the highest level, because you're still holding something back.

Giving That Hurts—Sacrifice

This is the top level. You're giving so much of your TEAM that it actually hurts. The cost is significant and uncomfortable. This level of relationship is Jesus's ultimate goal for family and guests in social dilemmas, and Jesus will never ask us to do something that he didn't already demonstrate. This is the *agape* love that Christ modeled:

- Romans 5:8—But God demonstrates his own love for us in this: While we were still sinners, Christ died for us.

> - John 3:16—For God so loved the world that he gave his one and only son that whoever believes in him will not perish but have eternal life.
> - John 15:13—Greater love has no one than this: to lay down one's life for one's friends.
>
> God's love for us required sacrifice. It cost him dearly.
>
> Level-4 relationships sound like this: regardless of the condition of the other person and regardless of my own condition, I will sacrifice for them. This is what Jesus is teaching about in Matthew 5:38–48. Go ahead and turn to that passage in your Bible and read it if that's what God is putting on your heart to do.

Regardless of the condition of the other person and regardless of my own condition, I will sacrifice for them.

When you know someone has sacrificed for you, it significantly increases the relationship. It's a game-changer. We also know that it's a different level of pain and hurt when someone is unwilling to sacrifice for you, isn't it? It breaks trust. It breaks relationship. When Jesus asked the rich, young ruler to break off his relationship with money, it was so that he could have a level-4 relationship with Jesus. Jesus would be on the throne of his heart, nothing else.

I want this to sink in for a second, because this may be an *ah-ha* moment for you. One of the main reasons why people are so lonely and disconnected these days is because we've lost the willingness and ability to sacrifice, and we feel it. What's the consequence? In a society where no one is willing to sacrifice, no one feels truly loved. There won't be any level-4 relationships, and "love" gets relegated to only levels 1 through 3. This continues to produce a society that seems to be growing exponentially in *selfish* and *self-protective* relationships, where people are wondering if even level-3—*selfless*—relationships are possible.

> In a society where no one is willing to sacrifice, no one feels truly loved.

Let's bring the concepts of TEAM and levels of relationship together. **Relationships strengthen or weaken based on the level of TEAM sacrifice that exists in that relationship.** I'm calling this your SQ—Sacrifice Quotient. It's likely that you already know about IQ and EQ, but when it comes to successful relationships, it's not only about your knowledge or intellectual ability (IQ), or how well you connect and understand emotions in yourself and other people (EQ). Those concepts are both important, but I believe that what is most critical is your relationship's SQ. The **SQ is the amount of mutual sacrifice over time in a relationship.** The amount of SQ will determine the strength of your relationship. In other words, your level of mutual sacrifice determines your level of relationship. This is not just from me. This is what God established and demonstrated. Mutual sacrifice is what is required for the greatest relationships. Did you catch that "mutual" part? If it's only one person who's sacrificing, we are back to levels 1 or 2, and those are not healthy relationships.

So what stops us from growing in our relationships? Growing our SQ? Any and all the parts of our TEAM that we are unwilling to give up. Whatever we are unwilling to sacrifice, God knows it will hinder relationship between him and us. This brings us back to the rich, young ruler. He was unwilling to sacrifice his money and, therefore, was unable to engage the level of relationship that Jesus wanted. Remember, it's not just about money per se; it's any heart distraction we are drawn to in our lives. Anything that lures our TEAM away from being Christ-centered. The young ruler's distracted heart drove his choice to walk away, and Jesus respected that choice.

I want to pause here one more time. We need to take a moment to see if God wants to put any relationships on your heart with respect to SQ. I'm going to ask God to show you a few things. Write down anything he puts on your heart. Don't rush this. Listening to God helps us walk at the pace of peace. Are there any relationships that you are struggling in right now or ones that you want to take to the next level?

Friend?

Spouse?

Coworker?

Classmate?

Teammate?

Family member?

Neighbor?

Now ask God to show you what level you are at right now in those relationships. Then ask him to show you where your next step of TEAM sacrifice should be.

Asking God these questions is a great exercise to do with him on a regular basis. I know for me, at least, it helps keep my heart aligned with God's goal of relationship. Unfortunately, I have also discovered in this process that the distracted path of the rich, young ruler is often closer to my heart than I would like to believe.

Let's get back to the story of the young ruler now to emphasize another point Jesus was trying to make. After the man walked away grieving, Jesus went on to explain how hard it is for a rich person to get into the kingdom of God, and he cracked a joke about a camel and the eye of a needle. He loved to use hyperbole, just to make sure he was clear. The difficulty for the rich is not because of money per se, because there were plenty of wealthy people in the church, including Joseph of Arimathea. The struggle is because of the security, trust, and hope that people find in money. Many rich individuals spend a lot of their TEAM focusing on their money instead of being willing to sacrifice it and depend on God. Any sacrifice they make to gain more money grows their relationship with their money. In essence, Jesus wants us to know that wherever we put our best TEAM will become a rival to God in our lives. It could be money, jobs, sex, sports, a girlfriend or boyfriend, a spouse, right or wrong behavior, a close friend, politics, a social cause, education, achievement, or even ourselves. On top of that, the higher the SQ we establish in those areas, the stronger that rivalry with God will be. It seems that we can turn almost anything into a rival to God in our hearts. In the rich, young ruler's case, even putting his security in trying to do everything right turned him away from God.

> *Wherever we put our best TEAM will become a rival to God in our lives.*

I want to show you one more cool thing that God is trying to do through this story. The literary context of the previous story in the Gospel of Mark sets up perfect irony. The previous story was about children coming to Jesus (Mark 10:13–16). How profoundly ironic is the kingdom of God? The children in the former story who possessed nothing were told by Jesus that they lacked nothing. This rich, young ruler who possessed everything was told by Jesus that he still lacked something! Only when he sacrificed and sold all he had, only when he became like a vulnerable child in a dependent relationship with God, would he possess all that he truly needed.

I really do believe that SQ is how we make or break relation-ships. God's goal is relationship, so we must take the *how* very seri-ously. To be equipped in the way of Jesus is to always be praying before and during our social dilemmas. It is doing whatever it takes to align our heart to God's goal of relationship, without any dis-tracting rivals.

Based on all that we have learned, let's add a bit more to Jesus's method for social dilemmas:

THE **JESUS** METHOD

STEP 1   Prayer

STEP 2A If family, then challenge and empower

STEP 2B If guest, then provide and respect

**If you are unsure as to whether they are family or guest, treat them as a guest.

Goal—Relationship with God and others

Prayerful Reflection

1. What is a new insight about the Jesus Method?
2. Is there a social dilemma in your life in which your heart has not wanted relationship?
3. What is challenging to you about SQ? What did you discover praying through that exercise in this chapter?
4. What questions do you have?
5. What specific relationship does God want you to be praying about?

CHAPTER 3

WITNESS

So far, we've covered the contextualization and goal of the Jesus Method. God's goal is always increased relationship. Last chapter we looked at a Jewish man who claimed to be a part of the family but ended up walking away as a guest. Now I want us to examine a social dilemma of a man who was a guest but walked away as a part of the family. The social dilemmas that we face in our lives come from both directions, so it will be helpful to observe how Jesus engaged it from a different context. In particular, I want us to take a closer look at the role that being a witness plays in the Jesus Method. Being a witness refers to someone who is experiencing something and sharing about it with others.

Let's set the scene. Jesus has just calmed a huge storm on the lake. It was a great show of power that led to fear in the disciples (Luke 8:24–25). As they are recovering from that experience, they arrive on the shore and find themselves in Gentile territory in the region of the Decapolis.

As he stepped out on shore, a man from the city who had demons met him. For a long time he had not worn any clothes, and he did not live in a house but in the tombs. When he saw Jesus, he cried out and fell down before him, shouting, "What have you to do with me, Jesus, Son of the Most High God? I beg you, do not torment me." (Luke 8:27–28 NIV)

This was quite the welcoming party for Jesus and his family, and immediately we notice that the demons inside the man were being a twofold witness. First, there was a clear declaration of who Jesus was. I always find it amazing how *non-confused* the spiritual realm is with Jesus's identity. We also see this in other parts of scripture when Jesus cast out demons. They were constantly declaring that he is the Christ (John 4:41). Evidently, though humanity has all kinds of questions, doubts, and confusion about who Jesus is, demons don't. Second, the demons were a witness of what they expected from power and authority. Their response indicates that they expected fear and torment, because that is what their master, Satan, does. Whenever someone has a different master than Jesus, power and authority will be linked with fear. This gives us insight on where the disciples were in their own faith journey. They had a similar fearful reaction to Jesus's show of power on the lake. Jesus responded to their fear with the question, "Where is your faith?" (Luke 8:25). Jesus's question is not about how powerful they thought he was. He was challenging them to connect his power to goodness instead of connecting it to fear. They were about to witness Jesus's power again, but this time, it was over the spiritual realm, not the natural realm. It was not over what was going on outside of people, but what was happening inside of them.

> *Whenever someone has a different master than Jesus, power and authority will be linked with fear.*

Jesus challenged his family to greater faith and relationship with himself and that they must understand that fear and faith do not mix. Jesus was teaching them that the purpose of power is to spread the gospel, the good news of God. God is both all-powerful and all-good. Jesus knew that if power and fear were inextricably linked in their minds, then their witness, their re-presentation of God, would be hindered. Fear always blocks people's relationship with God. When fear is present, full relationship with God can't be because his perfect love casts out all fear (1 John 4:18).

Fear always blocks people's relationship with God.

Back to the story:

> For Jesus had commanded the unclean spirit to come out of the man. (For many times it had seized him; he was kept under guard and bound with chains and shackles, but he would break the bonds and be driven by the demon into the wilds.) Jesus then asked him, "What is your name?" He said, "Legion," for many demons had entered him. They begged him not to order them to go back into the abyss. (Luke 8:29–31 NIV)

Jesus immediately started to provide for this guest as well as the surrounding region who had been terrorized by the man. Also notice the theme of power in this story that is continuing from the previous narrative of Jesus calming the storm. There is a clear hierarchy being established: demons (spiritual realm) are stronger than humanity (or whatever strength humanity can create—chains and shackles), but Jesus is stronger than the demons. Because power was linked to fear for the demons, they continued to beg with Jesus, knowing full well they dare not challenge his power and authority. Even in this pleading, the demons are a witness to the reality of eternal punishment. I can't imagine the look on the disciples' faces when this conversation was happening!

Jesus allowed the demons to go into a large herd of pigs that then rushed into the lake and drowned. When the herdsmen saw this show of power, they were filled with fear. The link between power and fear is clear in them as well. They ran away into the city and were witnesses to what had just happened, sharing it with the whole region.

> And the people went out to see what had happened. When they came to Jesus, they found the man from whom the demons had gone out, sitting at Jesus' feet, dressed and in his right mind; and they were afraid. Those who had seen it told the people how the demon-possessed man had been cured. (Luke 8:35–36 NIV)

Once again, in these guests, power was linked to fear. Those who had seen it were witnesses to the whole thing, sharing about it freely. Jesus had provided for all the guests. The man was healed completely, and the city and region were freed from being terrorized by this man. These are both incredibly good things! Now, the guests had the choice to link power to the goodness of Jesus or let fear continue to reign. Much like the rich, young ruler, we once again see that at the root of every social dilemma is a heart dilemma. *Who or what is on the throne of our hearts? What do we really want? What's the goal?* In this story, will fear rule or do these guests truly want relationship with God? "Then the whole throng of people of the surrounding region of the Gerasenes asked Jesus to leave them, for they were seized with great fear. So he got into the boat and returned" (Luke 8:37 NIV).

The townspeople made their choice. Choices are sacred, and regardless of how disappointing it had to be for Jesus and no matter how "wrong" they were in their decision, Jesus had no retaliation, no counterargument, no debate, and no further dialogue at all with them. He simply respected where they were in their faith, got back into the boat, and returned. What a tragedy!

I see this all the time in guests and family members alike. Fear can bully our hearts, guide us to doubt the goodness of God, and sow seeds of distrust. As a result, we might try to control a social dilemma in our lives or not trust God with the full outcome. Out of fear of failure, fear of the unknown, or fear that we might say the wrong thing, we forego trying to build relationship. I realize that is the easier thing to do, but don't let fear trick you into thinking that *easier* means *better*. God wants to help his family have faith over fear. We need to keep going to him to ask for more faith (Luke 17:5).

What else is happening in this story regarding fear, power, and the goodness of God? We see that healthy fear, awe, and reverence of God is in direct contrast to the unhealthy fear that's involved with worldly power. The people of the region had been afraid of the power of the demonized man, because not even the strongest among them or the chains and shackles could control him. Clearly, Jesus was stronger than the man, and so with an increase in power came an increase of fear because to them, power and fear were inseparable. They were afraid of what Jesus did instead of being in awe of who he was. Sound familiar? That's where the disciples were on the boat during the storm, when Jesus asked them where their faith was. Faith and fear do not mix. Family members don't ever need to be afraid. God is always with us, even until the end of the age (Matt. 28:20). His presence is our assurance, and that confidence can wage war against fear in our lives. God will continue to challenge any element of fear that resides in the family, empowering them through the Spirit to fearlessly desire to do the will of God the Father.

They were afraid of what Jesus did instead of being in awe of who he was.

That's where the healed man found himself. His fear was gone, and his faith was growing. He wasn't afraid of the power of Jesus. He was in awe of the identity of Jesus: "The man from whom the demons had gone out begged that he might be with him, but Jesus sent him away, saying, 'Return to your home, and declare how much God has done for you.' So he went away, proclaiming throughout the city how much Jesus had done for him (Luke 8:38–39 NIV).

Ah, I love this part of the story! There's more begging going on, but this time it's begging for relationship with Jesus. Jesus's opinion on what his next step should be differed from what the man wanted. This former demon-possessed guy was now a part of the family, which means Jesus moved into a new phase of his method. Though it caused disagreement, Jesus immediately challenged the man to go back home. Jesus was stepping up the SQ potential! Jesus then empowered the man to be a witness. Being a witness was the strategy that Jesus had for spreading the gospel to that whole region. That had to be tough for the man to hear, but he proved once again that furthering his relationship with God was his goal. He wanted God on the throne of his heart. He desired to do the will of God above and beyond his selfish wants and desires.

So, the man went off to be a witness for God in the whole region. You might say, "Of course this is what Jesus asked him to do, right? When you look at the seminary education of the man, how he had perfect attendance at church, including mission trips, his extravagant generosity, and his record of Godly character, he's a no-brainer candidate for being a witness for Christ!" Did you pick up on my sarcasm? Whatever God calls the family to do, he will equip the family to accomplish. Once you choose to be in the family of God, there are no other prerequisites for being a witness for God. Full throttle to being a witness is the strategy of Jesus, and that's what family members are empowered to do (Acts 1:8). Just in case someone in the family seems like they have nothing to do or don't know what their next step is, challenge them to be a witness. Of course, make sure you're being a witness as well; we can't have those "logs" creeping back up!

Whatever God calls the family to do, he will equip the family to accomplish.

We also see in this story that success for Jesus is at the pace of one relationship at a time. The masses chose to remain as guests, but the healed man chose to be family. Just like Jesus called his disciples by name, and how everyone who is in the family of God can recall a personal experience of encountering God, Jesus's goal is accomplished one relationship at a time. He challenged the man to go back to his home region and be a witness. We know this strategy worked in spreading the gospel because this same geographic area became a refuge for part of the early church during the first Jewish-Roman war (66–73 CE).

Success for Jesus is at the pace of one relationship at a time.

I mentioned it earlier, but I think it is important to bring up again. The juxtaposition of this demon-possessed man and the rich, young ruler demonstrates an opposite direction of the Jesus Method. The ruler went from claiming to be family to being a guest, but this troubled man goes from being a guest to becoming family. In every social dilemma situation, one relationship at a time, we must prayerfully discern the proper contextualization. Whether family or guest, we are committed to letting God meet them right there with an invitation to their next step in relationship. We can expect that somewhere in our dialogue we will have an opportunity to be a witness to what God has done in our own life. In addition, once someone joins the family, they are ready to be a witness right away.

We see an almost identical situation with a Samaritan woman whom Jesus met at a well at midday (John 4). After she accepted his invitation into the family, she immediately ran back into the town to be a witness for Christ. Jesus's strategy of her being a witness worked. Many Samaritans from that town believed in him because of the woman's testimony: "He told me all that I ever did" (John 4:39). This is the strategy that family members are empowered to carry out, one relationship at a time.

It's helpful to know that even though the disciples were shocked that Jesus would even be talking to a Samaritan woman—or the demoniac, for that matter—they would not have been surprised by the strategy of being a witness itself. The expectation of being a witness for God would have been well understood by the Jews. They already were accustomed to the concept from the prophet Isaiah.

"But you are my witnesses, O Israel!" says the LORD.
    "You are my servant.
You have been chosen to know me, believe in me,
    and understand that I alone am God.
There is no other God—
    there never has been, and there never will be.
I, yes I, am the LORD,
    and there is no other Savior.
First I predicted your rescue,
    then I saved you and proclaimed it to the world.
No foreign god has ever done this.
    You are witnesses that I am the only God," says the
    LORD. (Isa. 43:10–12)

For the family today, let's catch up on how being a witness is a meta-narrative throughout all of Scripture. It had a very early start in Genesis 2 with the *imago Dei*, as humanity was created in the image of God. There was the command to Adam and Eve to go out into all of the earth, *re*-presenting who God is everywhere they go. God scattered the people after the Tower of Babel and then gave a promise to Abraham's family of being a blessing to the whole world. In the New Testament, not only do we see Jesus overtly commission his family to go and make disciples of all nations, but then he follows that up with the Holy Spirit, who will empower the family to be witnesses: "But you will receive power when the Holy Spirit comes upon you. And you will be my witnesses, telling people about me everywhere—in Jerusalem, throughout Judea, in Samaria, and to the ends of the earth" (Acts 1:8).

Even in the end times in the book of Revelation, we see the importance of God's strategy for his family being witnesses. During the tribulation over a hundred thousand messianic Jews were witnesses throughout the world, empowered to invite as many people as they could into the family of God. There are also seminal moments in Revelation that involved the two witnesses of God. At first, they displayed incredible power, but then they were defeated, only to rise again from the dead as witnesses to the power and goodness of God. In addition, we are told that Satan himself was defeated in part by those who were being witnesses to who God is and what he had done:

> They triumphed over him
>> by the blood of the Lamb
>> and by the word of their testimony;
> they did not love their lives so much
>> as to shrink from death. (Rev. 12:11 NIV)

Being a witness always has been and always will be a part of God's strategy to form relationship, with him and each other.

I want to take a moment to make sure I'm being clear on this whole witness thing. The word *witness* in scripture is always in the noun form, never in the verb form. In other words, "witness" is not just something we do, it's who we are. And here's the thing: we're experts at being witnesses. In this day and age, most guests and family members are already fully equipped to be witnesses because of our experience with social media. Social media is a witness playground. One of the reasons why social media is so pervasive is because it connects to how humans are wired up to be witnesses. It's God's purpose for us. The question is not whether we are witnesses. It's who or what is the *object* of our witness. If someone follows us on social media, do they know who or what we follow? *Absolutely they do.* Whatever we post about is what we are a witness to. The evidence is right there. Being a witness is going to happen whether we're intentional about it or not.

To the family and the guests who are watching our lives, we are witnesses to who God is, what he does, and how he does it. As family members, when we enter social dilemmas, we are modeling God to people, regardless of our intentions. You might say, "That's not fair!" Well, there's very little about being a Christ-follower that's fair. There's certainly nothing fair about the cross of Christ. How we are witnesses to others in the middle of our social dilemmas may be the closest picture of who God is that they will ever see. So, let's make sure we are getting the Jesus Method locked in. God wants his family to be witnesses of him. It's not a suggestion; it's an expectation. This might be a good time to pause, pray, and see if there is anything that God wants to put on your heart about being a witness. You can ask God questions like this: Is there anything I am afraid of that is holding me back from being a witness? What am I a witness of right now on social media? How about in my face-to-face interactions? What is one experience of you, God, that you would like me to share with others?

Remember to write down anything that God is putting on your heart.

In order for us to be the most effective witness we can be, we must have ongoing experiences of God and ongoing sharing about him. It's not enough to just have one or the other. If we're experiencing God and not sharing, we're in danger of becoming spiritually obese. If we just share but don't have ongoing, relational experience with him, we're in danger of no longer being in tune with the Spirit. The latter didn't turn out well for Israel when they continued religious sharing and activities but no longer were experiencing the presence of God in the temple (Ezekiel 10). We don't want that to happen in our churches!

Another fascinating thing about being a witness is when social science catches up to God. In a courtroom, for example, what does a witness say? "I saw this happen to this person, and I am telling the court about it." At the core of being a witness are "I" statements. We know from the field of psychology and counseling that using "I" statements is the best chance of mitigating conflict among people: *I saw this, I felt this, I thought this when this thing happened.* Think about it. God's strategy to spread the good news of Christ across the planet is carried in the vehicle of "I" statements. This means that when social dilemmas arise, God's strategy of being a witness is the best method to prevent unnecessary conflict or volatility. God is good like that!

Now that we understand the importance of being a witness, let's talk about the two most common blocks that family members face about being a witness. The first one is all about the *content* of your testimony. I have heard people say all the time that they don't share their story because "it's not very good," "it's not as good as someone else's," "it's boring," or "it's not powerful enough." I'll admit. This is where I was for a long time in my life, and it's very common in family members who have grown up going to church. For me, all the testimonies that I ever heard at church or on videos were very dramatic, with rock-bottom moments or miraculous interventions. I would often think to myself, *I didn't have any of that. I hadn't killed anyone, been addicted to drugs or alcohol, gone to jail, or stolen a bunch of stuff, so my story is puny compared to those other people's. Who cares about my repentance for talking back to my parents, and the pride I felt when I compared myself to my classmates? That's nothing compared to hearing about some guy who was left for dead but then God showed up in a vision and changed his life. Personally, I'd rather hear more about the dead-come-back-to-life guy too!*

I call this *witness envy*, and I was saturated in it.

Witness envy is rampant in the family of God, and I believe it's stifling the Spirit's empowerment of each person's witness. It makes us feel unworthy, powerless, and less valuable than other family members. None of that is of God.

By the grace of God, he allowed me to see this in my own life. I was a professor at a local Christian university when I was asked to be a witness, to share my testimony at a chapel service. My thoughts just took off: *Uh oh, here we go. Everyone is going to be bored. There's nothing exciting about my story. People might think, "What's the big deal about God?" because of how pitiful my story is.* I was even tempted to spice it up a bit, which is a nice way of saying lie about it to make my story sound more dramatic. Did I mention that witness envy is dangerous? Witness envy caused me to want to hide the very thing that God promised to empower me to do. I was in a social dilemma, which meant my heart was in a dilemma. What did I really want? Did I really want to listen to the Word of God and then obey it, or not? Did I really want to take the next step of trust in God's and my relationship, or try to control the situation for what I thought would be a better outcome?

After praying about it, I said yes to the opportunity to share my story. I made it through step 1 of the Jesus Method. Before you give me any credit for that, you need to know that I still didn't think my witness would work. It was my fear weakening my relational connection with God. Yet he continued to challenge and empower me in this opportunity. He allowed me to have more faith than fear when I got on that stage.

I shared my story of growing up in the church, being part of a wonderful Christian family, asking a lot of questions, and then giving my life to Christ during confirmation class in sixth grade. After my decision to follow Jesus, I experienced change in my fears, temper, anxiety, and overly competitive spirit. I also talked about how God helped me to work through the pride that I had, thinking I was better than other people because I had "never really messed up in a big way." I spoke about the adventure that God had me on in my twenties and thirties, switching my careers multiple times and his guidance through unpredictable situations. All of this refined my dependency on him. I finished by expressing my genuine excitement about the journey ahead, daily trusting in God, simply listening and obeying and leaving the consequences up to him.

And then it happened. Right as I was wondering whether my story would have any impact at all, students came up to me in tears, thanking me for sharing my story. One of them who had a similar upbringing said to me, "I've never heard someone share a story like yours. I've never heard someone *make it* from a Christian home without having to fall off the wagon first." That person was seriously questioning whether kids in Christian homes could grow up to have real faith, because he had never heard anyone talk about it before. I had another student share with me that he had been questioning his faith for a long time. He was even considering purposely sinning in some major way just so that he would be able to have a "true" conversion experience after hitting rock bottom. Student after student stunned, affected, moved by God through the sharing of my story.

I very quickly realized that God was doing something beyond the facts of my story. God was empowering my witness, just like he had promised to do. It was powerful to see what God did as I was obedient to being a witness for him. That day changed everything for me when it comes to being a witness, and I can't tell you how free my soul feels now. Being a witness is not just about your testimony of conversion. It's about continuing to have both ongoing experiences of God and ongoing sharing about him. If you're in the family, I'm encouraging you to give God a chance to empower your witness. Don't let witness envy block your impact on those around you. You can pause and pray right now and ask God what that opportunity to be a witness looks like in your life. Like I was, I know you might be afraid to do this, but God is with you. Let him do what only he can do with your story. Every story matters!

Witness envy is the first block to being a witness, which is all about the *content* of your witness. However, the second block to being a witness is related to your *competency*. In our church, we talk about going and making disciples all the time, so when I bring up sharing one's faith in a conversation, I frequently see people stop making eye contact with me and shrug their shoulders. When I dig a little deeper into what's going on, I start to hear a disturbing pattern. They seem to understand the concept of being a witness, but then they say, "I don't know what to say," "I'm not very good at speaking about that sort of thing," "I don't know enough about God or the Bible," or "I'm afraid that people will get a bad impression of God if I can't answer people's questions." Though there are some content issues in these excuses, the primary focus is on competency. It's when you believe you don't have the ability to communicate what God has done or is doing in your life. Even if you are grateful or excited about your story, you have a block on competently communicating it.

If this is where you're at, you're not alone. Moses knows what you're experiencing (Exodus 3), John and Peter were just ordinary men who surprised everyone when God empowered their witness (Acts 4:13), and Paul had times of almost boring people to death with his teaching (Acts 20:9–12). Yet all these people were incredible witnesses of God, and God used their stories to affect the world! God wants you to succeed at being a witness even more than you want to succeed. It's why God promises to empower you. The reality is none of us is competent on our own. However, with God empowering you, you *will* have an impact on those around you.

> As a witness, you especially will have influence on the two or three people you see two or three times a week. I call these groups of people your impact circles, because God has already given you potential impact in their lives.

If fear ever tries to bully your heart, remember the demon-possessed guy. He certainly sets the bar really low for the knowledge, experience, and competency that is required for being a witness. Not only can God use your witness for his purposes, but he also can't wait to empower your witness. Your story matters! God wants to empower your ongoing story of how you're experiencing God so that you can share it with others. Give God a chance to use the story he is writing through your life. It'll be one of the best things you've ever done in your relationship with him.

Let's take a moment to pray about that:

Lord, we come before you, and we are reminded that you were a comprehensive witness to the Father. You even said that you can't do anything on your own; you only do what you see the Father doing. You were such a complete witness that you even told your disciples that when they had seen you, they had seen the Father. Lord, please show me any area of witness envy that I might have that is making me timid with my story. [Pause for reflection.] *Lord, please put on my heart any doubts about my competency that I need to hand over to you.* [Pause for reflection.] *Lord, help my heart be committed to wanting to be your witness. I'm trusting in your promises to empower me as I share with others how I'm experiencing you. Love you. In Jesus's name I pray, amen.*

Before we move on to the next chapter, let's review what we have added to Jesus's method:

THE **JESUS** METHOD

STEP 1   Prayer

STEP 2A   If family, then challenge and empower

STEP 2B   If guest, then provide and respect

**If you are unsure as to whether they are family or guest, treat them as a guest.

Goal—Relationship with God and others

Pace—One relationship at a time

Strategy—Being a witness

Prayerful Reflection

1. What is a new insight about the Jesus Method?
2. Is there an area of your life where God wants to empower you to be a witness?
3. What is challenging to you about being a witness? Do you wrestle more with witness envy or questions about your competency?
4. What questions do you have?
5. What specific relationship does God want you to be praying about?

CHAPTER 4

SOCIAL MEDIA

The strategy of being a witness with the goal of relationship is the way of Jesus. Jesus said that if you have seen him, you have seen the Father. He was a witness to the Father, and his goal was to grow relationships with people at the pace of one relationship at a time. In this way, everyone has the opportunity to experience a personal connection with God, fully known and fully chosen.

Of course, people can choose to reject God. We have already seen that with the rich, young ruler, and Jesus let him walk away. The eternal consequence for people who walk away from God is a sticking point for many family members when it comes to social dilemmas. I have heard them say, "If hell's the reality of the state of this life and forever for those guests, why wouldn't we do everything possible to argue and convince someone to follow Jesus?"

Because Jesus didn't do that and we're following him, not the other way around.

I've heard family members and guests alike ask, "But where's Jesus's compassion for the lost if he lets people walk away?" I love their heart in this question, but just because he lets someone walk away doesn't mean his heart isn't breaking. We see his heart shatter when he approached Jerusalem for one of the last times. He was mourning the loss of so many who refused to believe in him (Matthew 23; Luke 19). Clearly, engaging social dilemmas with the goal of avoiding heartbreak or rejection is not the method of Jesus. We certainly are not trying to cause such suffering, but people will make choices, and choices have consequences. That's why we must get *how* we navigate social dilemmas correct, and then we leave the consequences up to God.

Along this same line of false-compassion thinking, I often experience family members treating guests as family members. They are challenging them and trying to empower them when they should be providing for their needs. Why does this happen? Many times it's because the family wants the guest to have relationship with God so badly that they stop providing for their needs or stop respecting their choice. They might even think, *If I just challenge them a bit more, maybe argue from a different angle, they would finally get it!* As soon as we stop following the Jesus Method in social dilemmas, regardless of our heart's intentions, we start being a false witness. False witness? Ouch! That one hurt me, too, when God put that on my heart. It was convicting for me, and though conviction is always out of God's kindness (Rom. 2:4), it isn't always comfortable. I want people to have a full life, but oftentimes, I've realized that I want it more than they do. As I've tried to follow the Jesus Method, I've had to learn how to walk away or let them walk away. It's actually the most compassionate thing I can offer at that point. Doing what Jesus did is always the most loving thing to do.

As soon as we stop following the Jesus Method in social dilemmas, regardless of our heart's intentions, we start being a false witness.

This whole discussion about compassion, hell, and respecting people's faith choices reminds me of a situation that may come up in a romantic relationship. *Hold on, stay with me here!* Let's say there's a woman who is living her own life with the usual ups and downs, and a guy comes along who's really into her. He's not creepy; he just genuinely cares about her and wants to have a relationship. She brushes him off because he's not her type. He's not ready to give up, so he brings her gifts, tries to spend some time with her, writes her notes, and encourages her every time he's in her presence. Even though he's being very respectful, she's just not into him. She wants to do her own thing, and he's starting to be a distraction, which is annoying. However, she hasn't told him completely to leave her alone because every now and then it's nice to have someone care about her, make her life a little easier, and pick her up when she's having a bad day. That's all she wants from him, nothing more. As time goes on, he stays diligent, so even though she's pulling away most of the time, he continues to find opportunities to express his love for her. This goes on for quite some time, until it's just too much for her to handle, and she decides to be honest with him. He's just not what she's looking for. She wants different things in life than he does, and they're not going in the same direction. He's a nice guy but not her type. She wants him to leave her alone, stop pursuing her, and let her live her own life.

Think about this moment.

The most loving thing that man can do is honor her choice. He needs to leave her alone, no matter how he feels about her and regardless of the bad consequences that may come from her choice. He has been clear, and the invitation for relationship had been given more times than he could remember. In her heart, she has chosen what she truly wants, and that choice sets a direction that leads to a destination away from him. Heartbroken, the man respects her choice and leaves her alone.

That's where we find ourselves with God in this social dilemma process. Hell is not somewhere that God forces people to go to. God lets them go. They have been clear about what they want, and it's not a relationship with him. He's not their type. They want to live their own lives. Eternity is when you live out the consequences of what you have wanted in this life. Heaven is full of people in love with God and wanting full relationship with him. You get heaven when a full relationship with Jesus is what you really want. Every social dilemma is rooted in a heart dilemma. What do we really want? We all will get in the next life what our hearts have really wanted in this life. It's crazy to think about, but we actually get to choose how we want to spend eternity. In fact, we already are choosing it in our hearts every single day (Prov. 4:23). God refuses to lower the bar on true love. True love requires choice, and we are the ones who get to choose. Oh, how sacred our choices are!

Jesus chose to sacrifice to provide an invitation to a level-4 relationship with God now and forever. This is incredibly good news for the family, and it's great news for the guests because they're invited too! Jesus doesn't want a single person to perish (2 Pet. 3:9). The family needs to keep inviting the guests into that relationship by providing for their needs and being a witness.

The family can be witnesses face to face as well as online. Social media is a powerful tool to invite people into their next step of relationship with God. That brings us to another social dilemma that Jesus navigated. This one involves social media. Obviously, this was different technology than social media in the digital space today, but it's still similar in nature. In biblical times, some event would happen, people would share about it in their private and public spaces, and news of it would spread quickly all over the community. *Sound familiar?*

As we enter this topic, it's important to realize that digital is not good or bad per se. It's like a brick, which can help build a house or really hurt someone. It all depends on how it's used. The responsibility of the effect it causes rests solely on the person holding the brick. It's not the brick's fault! Once again, it's not just *what* something is but *how* it is used that's critical.

Yes, digital is new, but advances in technology are not. They just look different in different eras. Technology is when science is applied for practical purposes. In biblical times, letters were amazing technology, resembling contemporary tech in several ways. For example, Paul would write a letter and then send it to someone by a courier, trade route, or ship. He wouldn't get to defend, explain, articulate, or add inflection or tone to it. It was like an extremely slow text message. In addition to these private letters, events happened on broader social platforms, and word of them spread crazy fast. We've already covered some of these events: Jesus's miracle of the feeding of the 5,000, John the Baptist getting killed, and the demoniac. What we begin to realize is that though the information traveled a different speed, the nature of the information carried the same power as present-day social media.

Let's look at a social media event in Jesus's day and see whether he applied his method to it. If he did, we should be able to apply it on our social media today.

> At dawn he appeared again in the temple courts, where all the people gathered around him, and he sat down to teach them. The teachers of the law and the Pharisees brought in a woman caught in adultery. They made her stand before the group and said to Jesus, "Teacher, this woman was caught in the act of adultery. In the Law Moses commanded us to stone such women. Now what do you say?" They were using this question as a trap, in order to have a basis for accusing him. (John 8:2–6)

We have all kinds of social dilemmas here. There is clearly a double standard for women in this story, which was the norm in those days. A strict following of the Law of Moses would have brought out both the man and woman involved to be stoned to death. Adultery always takes two. The religious leaders came with bad intentions, and their hearts were decidedly against a relationship with Jesus. This dilemma was playing out in social media. The southern steps of the temple were perhaps the most public space that existed in Jerusalem. It was happening at the end of the Festival of Shelters, so there was a huge crowd and everybody was watching. They were ready to witness the showdown of the ages and then share about it with everyone who was missing it. Like some of our current social media situations, people often enter the digital space with unwholesome intentions. They have an agenda or a point of view that they are committed to conveying, regardless of the cost.

Before moving on in the story, let's look at what we know about the two sides of this social dilemma. The Pharisees were trying to trap Jesus by having him say something is right that the Law clearly said is wrong. Notice their emphasis on *what* is right and wrong in this scenario. That emphasis is already a clue that the Pharisees missed the goal of God. However, they did get something right about Jesus. Somewhere along the line, they picked up that Jesus seemed to always be full of grace. Here was an opportunity where if Jesus chose to be full of grace, it would come back to bite him, or so they thought. This was as high of stakes as it got: capital punishment. They knew that Jesus must show his true colors here. It was the perfect trap because they believed that full grace and full truth could not coexist. There was clarity in the rights and wrongs of the Law, and *how* it was interpreted and applied according to God's original heart was just not that important to them. The Law was from Moses after all, and there was no man higher than Moses.

Oops—they got that one wrong.

One of the hermeneutics that can be used when studying the Gospels is that Jesus is a better Moses. This lens through which to view and interpret scripture insists that the New Covenant (Jesus's forgiveness of sins) is superior to the Old Covenant (the Law). The way of Jesus is a better representation of the kingdom of God on Earth than the Law ever was. We see this play out right here in this story. It's the Law of Moses versus the heart of Jesus. It seems that we are back to rights versus relationship. Jesus was going to establish once again that relationship is a higher priority than what is right or wrong. Another way of saying this is that pursuing relationship with God is the rightest thing someone can do. That's why it's always the goal of God. What the religious leaders hadn't discovered yet is that Jesus was the first fulfillment of Jeremiah's prophecy of the Law being written on our hearts (Jer. 31:33). Our relationship with God sets the foundation for what is right and what is wrong.

Everyone in the crowd, including the woman caught in adultery, already knew the answer to the Pharisees' question: stone the woman. It's what the Law required. In her mind, there was zero chance of coming out of this alive. This was her death march. Most likely, this was not the first time the crowd had seen a stoning, and it's likely that many of them participated in one in the past. In this test of what's right and what's wrong, it seemed to be a no-brainer, a lob for Jesus to get it right.

Let's think about this from a social media perspective. Anything that gets posted in today's social media is instant, permanent, and global. Social media is like that brick we discussed earlier. The responsibility rests in the one posting on it. The woman caught in adultery was brought out into a very social platform. Her behavior was now out there in an instant. They all saw her. Her situation was permanent and global. To this day, all around the world, we are talking about her story. What we are about to see is that Jesus's response was also instant and permanent, and it went global.

This trap is what the Pharisees wanted. This was the win they were after. You can almost hear them cheering on Jesus: "Jesus, just say it; take a stance! Call it what it is. She's a sinner, she should be stoned, throw the book at her!" Can you sense the confidence in their hearts on the authority of what is right and wrong? There's no dilemma in their hearts at all! It's clear that judgment, punishment, and retaliation were their goals. It's what the Pharisees wanted! They wanted to get their seal of approval that knowing *what* is right and wrong gave them the right to judge others.

Have you ever felt this kind of pressure to take a stance on certain issues in social media? All your friends and followers are pushing you to do it. What is right and wrong seems obvious, and if you don't take a stand, they might start to question all kinds of things about you. There can be a pressure to respond to what seems to be blatantly wrong or clearly right, and to do so as soon as possible so that people can make an accurate judgment on your position. Are you still with "us" or are you with "them"? Wow—it can escalate very quickly, can't it?

Jesus was in the same predicament. The Pharisees had made their move. Now Jesus was on the clock. What was he going to do? Where did he stand? People were wondering, *Is he with us righteous people or with those sinners?*

Jesus bent down and started to write on the ground with his finger. I can imagine the crowds asking themselves, *What is Jesus doing? Why is he taking so long? We all know what the right thing to do is!"* Here's the scene: "When they kept on questioning him, he straightened up and said to them, 'Let any one of you who is without sin be the first to throw a stone at her.' Again, he stooped down and wrote on the ground" (John 8:7–8).

Wow! *What just happened? What did Jesus do?*

Jesus refused to cave to the pressure or enter into the nitpicky right-or-wrong argument. Instead, he elevated the situation to the higher goal of relationship. He's brilliant! Anyone without sin throw the first stone. Has anybody not broken their relationship with God? Go ahead, you can throw a stone at her.

Jesus refused to cave to the pressure or enter into the nitpicky right-or-wrong argument.

It got really quiet. The stipulation for throwing a stone pierced people's hearts, and everyone suddenly stopped looking for any stones: "At this, those who heard began to go away one at a time, the older ones first, until only Jesus was left, with the woman still standing there. Jesus straightened up and asked her, 'Woman, where are they? Has no one condemned you?' 'No one, sir,' she said" (John 8:9–11a).

I love it when God pulls out the question of asking where someone is, when he already knows the answer. It's always a flashback to the garden of Eden, and God loves to do it when people are hiding in sin. This woman had everything brought to the light. There was no place for her to hide, yet she was the only one remaining in Jesus's presence. He was the only one with the right to condemn her and throw a stone, but that's not why he came into the world. He came to save people just like her (John 3:17). "'Then neither do I condemn you,' Jesus declared" (John 8:11a).

Jesus is impressively consistent with his method. His goal is always relationship. The woman was a guest, so he provided for what she needed, cared for her, protected her, saved her from death, offered her grace, and invited her into a restored relationship with God. He took steps to recover her human dignity despite whatever choices she may have made. She clearly had a list of wrongs in her life, but his offer of relationship trumped that list. That's what grace does.

Where did everyone else go?

Jesus never said anyone had to leave. Much like the rich, young ruler, they were unwilling to give up what they had on the throne of their hearts. It wasn't money this time. It was their prideful judgment, zeal, and obsession for being right. They had elevated what was right and wrong over how to form relationship. Jesus finished his method and respected their choice to leave. He did not chase down, argue, debate, or retaliate against any of them. He let them go, fully knowing the consequences of their choice. Their hearts had decided what they truly wanted. They claimed to be family, but they walked away as guests. It had to break Jesus's heart to watch them go. Jesus's choice continued to solidify his commitment to his method, including honoring people's choice to not choose him.

We, too, must trust that following the Jesus Method in our social media will have similar results. Yes, some people might be upset and unfollow you or unsubscribe from your channel because your priority of relationship frustrates them. Others will feel seen and heard by God because of your commitment to prioritize relationship, providing for the needs of others. Sometimes prioritizing relationship can be misinterpreted as agreeing with or condoning someone else's behavioral choices. Jesus addressed that misunderstanding too.

Though Jesus chose to provide grace for the adulterous woman, did that mean he agreed with her or condoned her sin? *No.* Jesus knew that adultery breaks relationships, destroys families, and violates covenant. Jesus did not tolerate, agree with, or accept sin. He knew the wages of sin were death (Rom. 6:23). It's why he went on to sacrifice his life to break the power of sin and death once and for all. That's how strongly Jesus is against sin—all sin. There's nobody you'll ever meet who is more against sin than Jesus, and there's nobody you'll ever meet who is more for people than Jesus.

Jesus did not tolerate, agree with, or accept sin.

The outcome of this story teaches us something very important that we can hold onto during our own social dilemmas. Jesus demonstrates that caring is not condoning. Caring for someone, helping them have human dignity, protecting them from hatred or abuse is not the same thing as condoning whatever sin may be present in their life. Providing is not permission. Providing for someone's needs does not necessarily mean you give permission for their sinful behavior.

Caring is not condoning.

It wasn't that Jesus agreed with her sin or was just going to accept her sin. This was not some stance about tolerance. She was a guest, and Jesus knew relationship needed to be provided *first*. This woman was experiencing a highly traumatic situation, in which shame and hatred were heaped on her. Jesus provided a safe, personal conversation that would allow her to feel invited into a relationship. We see how his heart for relationship opened her heart for how he closed the conversation: "Go now and leave your life of sin" (John 8:11b).

Providing is not permission.

The Pharisees were wrong. All grace and all truth can coexist. His name is Jesus, and that combination is essential in his method of navigating social dilemmas. It's also essential in how we must engage our social dilemmas. With full grace, Jesus offered full truth. The Law was written on his heart. The *how* took precedence over the *what*. Both were communicated, but their order was critical. The goal was relationship, and once that family relationship began, he moved into challenging and empowering this woman to a new life away from all that sin.

One of my friends, Dr. Bob Laurent, who is a teaching pastor at our church, says it like this: "Grace without truth lies; truth without grace kills." Grace without truth would have lied to this woman. Sure, Jesus saved the day in that moment, but what would her life be like later? Would she have gone back to the affair? After all, she got away with it the last time, and it's doubtful these Pharisees would try that stunt again as long as Jesus was around. Maybe she would have thought, *I guess it was OK. Maybe the Law had been interpreted incorrectly all these years. Maybe the Law gives me what I want if I just do some mental gymnastics and provide a new interpretation that fits what I want.* In social dilemmas, we must not simply show grace, form relationship, and then leave out the truth. That's lying.

However, we must be cautious of going to the extreme in the other direction.

Truth without grace would have killed this woman, quite literally. If Jesus had thrown the first stone, they all would have jumped in. Even if it did not escalate to that, had Jesus just thrown the truth at her without grace-filled relationship, she would have walked away full of shame and condemnation without a connection to Jesus. Death is not just the absence of life someday in the future. Death is disconnection from he who is life, right now. She would have left the scene spiritually dead. Unfortunately, this is what often happens when well-meaning Christians enter social dilemmas with a different goal than God. It reminds me of what I said earlier in the book: when we don't know the way of Jesus, we weaponize the truth of Jesus.

Death is not just the absence of life someday in the future.
Death is disconnection from he who is life, right now.

Navigating these intense social dilemmas is extremely difficult. This is a good time to remind ourselves that the family can do nothing apart from God. Independence from God is never the aim of the family; living *in dependence* on God is the target. God has warned us over and over, including in John 15, that we must live in a state of dependency on God to do anything worthwhile. Our social dilemmas are incredibly challenging because they engage us physically, mentally, spiritually, and emotionally. Do not try the Jesus Method on your own. Even Jesus didn't try that (John 5:19). We must remain humble and reliant on the Spirit of God to help us through each step.

In the same spirit of humility, let's ask where we find ourselves in this social dilemma of the woman caught in adultery. I know I've already said it, but when we read the Bible, we must be humble enough to let it read us back: "Search me, God, and know my heart; test me and know my anxious thoughts. See if there is any offensive way in me and lead me in the way everlasting" (Ps. 139:23–24 NIV).

Some of us can relate to the Pharisees. In full transparency, maybe we have intentionally put someone on the hot seat, calling them out publicly for all to see. This could be in person or online. We might even feel justified in our actions, believing it was right to call out their wrong choices.

So did the Pharisees.

Perhaps for us, though, it's under the guise of "being real," "transparency," "honesty," or "not hiding what I really think." We might say to ourselves, *Someone needs to stand up and say it! I'm not afraid to say hard things or do the dirty work to contend for the faith, to stand up for what's right and what's wrong!* Be careful. Our hearts might be in a dilemma. We must make sure our hearts are aligned with God's heart for relationship with people.

When comparing the Pharisees with Jesus, we see an interesting pattern taking place. When leaders care about power, they make things public. When leaders care about people, they make things personal.

> *We must make sure our hearts are aligned with God's heart for relationship with people.*

Notice that Jesus took this situation out of the big gathering context and brought it into a one-on-one conversation. Jesus knew this was not a public situation but a personal one. Everything that needed to be said didn't have to be said in a large gathering context. Jesus certainly modeled that level of intentionality, but unfortunately, Christians often fail to make that adjustment.

I will admit that pastors often are one the biggest culprits of this. Sometimes pastors have an overzealousness or urgency to talk about a particular sin or hot-topic issue that they know a few people are experiencing. This situation can cause well-meaning pastors to make what should have been a personal conversation a public one. I get it. As a pastor, I often feel the pressure that I only have a limited amount of time with people to preach and communicate the truth of what is right and what is wrong. But then I remember, so did Jesus! Yet he stayed committed to his method, which was at the pace of one relationship at a time, and often resulted in way more personal conversations than public declarations about people's sins. I have learned that as the controversy level of a topic increases, so should my level of relationship with the person or audience. High levels of controversy require high levels of relationship for relational growth to still be possible.

When I have violated this connection that Jesus modeled and have spoken controversial truth without the required level of relationship, it has always ended with less relationship, not more. It poured fuel on the raging fire of people overemphasizing *what* is right and wrong. The people who agree with me celebrate passionately online and in the room, and those who don't agree are angered, frustrated, ashamed, and disillusioned. Disunity and division grow at a rapid pace. Power enters the space, and fear comes right behind it. I ask myself, *For what purpose?* I've never heard people who disagree with me change their mind and desire more relationship with God and me after such a public display of rightness. I've also never had those agree with me become more humble and guest focused because of those declarative moments. It seems that though what I say may be completely right, I get the goal completely wrong. Increasing relationship with God is *always* the goal.

As a result, this is what I have said many times to those who may be disgruntled about the absence of teachings on a few controversial sins from our weekend platform: "Just because we're not having this conversation from that stage doesn't mean that the conversation isn't happening." Life groups, discipleship classes, and discussions over coffee are much better venues for certain conversations. In these personal settings, dialogue about truth can occur, grace can be demonstrated, and people can experience being seen and heard in a way that invites them into relationship. Yet some may still argue, "But how will the people know the truth about these sins unless you preach about them?" My response is this: "That's where you and I come in and every member of the family comes in—each of us forming relationship and following the Jesus Method, one relationship at a time."

Jesus demonstrated that the level of controversy determines the level of relationship required. Though it may be inconvenient to many of our schedules, and more socially awkward at times, this is what we see Jesus consistently model. As my wife, a brilliant, licensed mental health counselor, often says, "It's only awkward until it isn't." In addition, it's helpful to remember that any sacrifice we make for personal conversations is an opportunity to raise the SQ in that relationship. We are back to the goal of God!

Here's the caution if you find yourself resonating with creating public controversies like the Pharisees. Remember, when the family follows the way of the Pharisees, it becomes clear to everyone else that our faith is more about power than about growing relationship. Let God meet you where you are, in all your frustration and passion for truth and justice. He is committed to both of those too, and his way is through relationship. We must be careful with how we declare truth. We can very quickly start sounding more like the Pharisees than Jesus.

Though some of us may connect well to the Pharisees, others of us relate more to the woman caught in adultery. We may have experienced times in our lives when we felt shame and embarrassment. Perhaps we had justified our sin in some way, making excuses for the choices we were making, or maybe we were just afraid that someone would find out, so we just kept hiding. Maybe you're still hiding. You know what it's like to hide, not make eye contact, and wish it would all go away. Maybe you've been where she was: caught, busted. There was no way out, and you knew that your life was essentially over, or perhaps that's your fear if you ever confess. Maybe you have some beliefs that are different than your family at home or your church family, and you're trying to hide them the best that you can and there's significant fear there.

This may be resonating with you, and you might be thinking, *Sure, I'd hope that people would treat me like Jesus did, with all grace and all truth while genuinely inviting me into restored relationship. Just one problem with that hope. When I look around at the church or Christians in general, that's not the vibe I get, and I'm pretty sure that's not how it would all go down.*

It's a dilemma, and you feel stuck and all alone. I get it, and you're not the only one.

If that's you right now, I need you to know what's true. Jesus can meet with you right there, right now, just like he did with the woman in this story. Jesus is not bound by space or time. He sees you, he knows you, and he would love to talk with you about this. Put this book down, and carve out time to meet with Jesus. Trust me. He's been looking forward to this moment for a long time because he loves you so much. He has so much restored relationship to invite you into. There's new life ahead of you through him. Believe it!

I want to take a moment to pray for all those who just chose to put this book down and meet with Jesus one on one right now.

Lord, we pray that you will be true to your promise to be close to the broken-hearted and that you came for those who know that they need you. Please bless each person meeting with you that they would experience your presence in a profound way. Whatever their next step is in relationship with you, we pray that they hear it clearly and have the courage to obey. In Jesus's name, amen.

Here is the caution if you find yourself resonating with the woman caught in adultery: make sure you don't project the Pharisees' reaction onto God.

Here is the caution if you're part of the family and someone caught in their sin is right in front of you: Strive to imitate the model of Jesus in every way. Be quick to listen, slow to speak, and slow to anger, remembering that anger does not produce the righteousness of God (Jas. 1:19–20). It's truly an honor for the Holy Spirit to entrust you with the brokenness of another. It's a privilege for God to choose to work through you to provide for someone else. It might be a listening ear, a shoulder to cry on, or the encouragement you can give that God sees them. With God's help, lean into that moment with care and compassion.

Sometimes we're like the one caught in sin, sometimes we're like the ones blatantly and publicly calling people out, but admittedly, many times we're like the ones standing around in the crowd. We are watching and listening, ready to be a witness to what is happening or chime in with our own opinions. Like the crowd, we see the sides of this social dilemma starting to take shape, and we can land on one side or the other. We might be thinking, *That's right, she deserves it. I knew she was trouble. Let her have it, Jesus.* Or we might want to say, "Who are these hypocrites to judge her? We see what they do when they're not in their fancy clothes. How do they really know what happened, and where's the man in this scenario?"

Don't think that this story just ended there. Who was in the temple courts? Who joined the parade as the Pharisees dragged this woman to Jesus? This was seen and talked about immediately, and then as people left the festival, they were witnesses to it all the way back home. We can't check the analytics and measure the digital footprint of reactions, shares, or comments, but it went viral.

In many of the social dilemmas we face, especially in the digital space, we're like this crowd. My caution, if you're resonating with being in the crowd, is don't be passive. Don't just sit back and take in what is happening and then share about it as soon as possible.

Engage the Jesus Method at whatever level you can. It might be as simple as growing in relationship with someone else in the crowd as you discuss what happened. Keep being challenged to actively familiarize yourself with what Jesus did and how he did it. Many times, this will lead you to an invitation to have a more personal conversation with someone, just like Jesus did, because the family cares about people, not power.

Let's look closer at Jesus's heart in this dilemma. It's clear that Jesus cared more for the woman than he hated the situation. His heart for her was greater than his disgust of her sin. I can't imagine how much Jesus hates evil (Rom. 12:9)—the very thing that breaks relationship with God, and what is constantly seeking to steal, kill, and destroy all that Jesus loves (John 10:10). Yet Jesus loves even more than that. Instead of defending himself in this situation, Jesus defended the woman while also defending the goal of relationship. Importantly, he did not defend what she did. He defended who she was made to be. He will always defend the opportunity to restore relationship with God. That's the goal. Once relationship was formed with the woman, he was able to challenge her about her sin. This is like the original ten commandments that came from God's loving relationship with his people. From his heart, he gave them boundaries to protect their relationship with God and with each other. It is from relationship in the family that we can challenge and empower each other. Relationship comes first, and then comes "leave your life of sin." Jesus didn't guilt her or condemn her into it, but with grace, he loved her toward her next step in growing relationship with God.

It's clear that Jesus cared more for the woman than he hated the situation. His heart for her was greater than his disgust of her sin.

Whether it was social media 2,000 years ago or the social media of today, God is all about inviting people into relationship. All of what we have discussed in this chapter can be applied directly to our interactions on social media. In addition, I want to pass on a filter for making decisions on what to put on social media. Think of it as a practical implementation of the Jesus Method. It's always helpful to think before you speak.

It's also helpful to THINK before you post. Ask yourself these questions before you make something instant, permanent, and global:

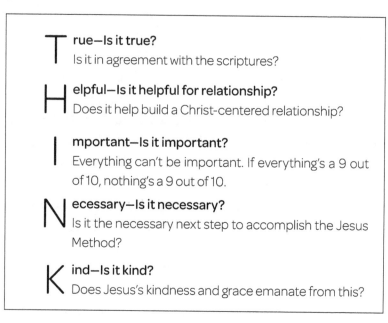

T rue—Is it true?
Is it in agreement with the scriptures?

H elpful—Is it helpful for relationship?
Does it help build a Christ-centered relationship?

I mportant—Is it important?
Everything can't be important. If everything's a 9 out of 10, nothing's a 9 out of 10.

N ecessary—Is it necessary?
Is it the necessary next step to accomplish the Jesus Method?

K ind—Is it kind?
Does Jesus's kindness and grace emanate from this?

This simple idea to THINK before posting has helped me so many times!

Prayerful Reflection

1. What is a new insight about the Jesus Method?
2. Which group of people in this story do you resonate with the most? To which cautions are you most vulnerable?
3. Are there any places in your social media feeds where you are not modeling Jesus?
4. What is challenging to you about pursuing personal conversations over public declarations?
5. What questions do you have?
6. What specific relationship does God want you to be praying about?

CHAPTER 5

CONTENDING FOR THE FAITH!

W e have taken a thorough journey into Jesus's method for navigating social dilemmas. It's usually at about this point that many people voice some discontentment. Perhaps the biggest contention that I have run into when laying out the Jesus Method is this: "Ted, what about contending for the faith?" I have heard the phrase "contending for the faith" used and misused repeatedly in the past few years with regards to social dilemmas. It's critical that we take a closer look at the meaning of this phrase, used only once in the entire Bible. The phrase comes from what has become one of my favorite books of the Bible on social dilemmas: the book of Jude.

I invite you to put this book down for a few minutes and read through the whole book of Jude. It's only one chapter, so it won't take too long! Try to read it through the lens of the Jesus Method and write down any insights that you gain along the way. What is the tone of the book? How does it compare with what we have already seen with Jesus in social dilemmas?

Now that you've read through Jude, let's take a deeper dive into it together and see what else God may have for us.

The name Jude is translated as Judas in the Greek, which connects the author to the biological family of Jesus. By all accounts, it seems like the author of this book is the half-brother of Jesus. Jude grew up with Jesus, but like his brother James, Jude didn't believe in Jesus as Messiah until after Easter. He was a guest until after the resurrection, when he became family. Quite literally, Jesus's own nuclear family was a daily social dilemma!

Right away in this book, Jude declared his family status by identifying Jesus as Lord and Master of his life. The language in Jude's introduction means that he most likely was talking to Messianic Jews. Since this letter is addressed to the family, what should we expect according to the Jesus Method? We should expect challenging and empowering encouragement to do the will of the Father. There will be discussion about guests in here, but the Holy Spirit is contextualizing this message for the family. Furthermore, Jude's literary triads emphasize that these instructions are for past, present, and future family members. The sovereignty that God has over time and space helps Christians today receive this social dilemma message as if it was written for us—because it was!

This book is essential in understanding the Jesus Method because it is a real, live demonstration of the process being walked out by a leader in the church, someone who was once a guest but now a part of the family. Jude would have empathy for the guest and a deep gratitude and love for the family. As current members of the church family, this book meets us right where we are, trying to live out the Jesus Method in a contentious world.

I love how early in this book Jude admitted that he didn't really want to enter this dilemma. He would much rather talk about the common faith and salvation that unites the family. It's the same with us today; so many times we don't want to have these conflictual conversations because social dilemmas are uncomfortable, inconvenient, and sometimes scary. Yet just like Jesus, Jude did not quit, and neither should the family. He activated Jesus's method to address an urgent dilemma that was developing.

I remember reading this book and asking the question, "What could be more urgent than talking about salvation and common faith?"

We need to go back to John 17 to answer this question. Jesus's largest concern as he was about to be turned over to be crucified was not something doctrinal or some theological right and wrong; it was disunity in the family. So, since that was one of Jesus's largest concerns, we see the Holy Spirit addressing it in the early church as well. What the early church had in common and what unified them was what Jude was eager to write about—namely, salvation. Unity does not mean we agree on everything; it means there is something higher, stronger, and more foundational than our agreements, disagreements, and opinions. We are united by our common need for Jesus. It is our salvation in Christ that unifies the family.

What's so urgent that Jude can't talk more about salvation? Jesus's largest concern—the threat of disunity—is on the rise.

Over what?

Contending for the faith.

There it is. That's the phrase!

That's what I hear Christians talking about all over the place. "Ted, I'm just contending for the faith!" Jude is where that phrase comes from, and unfortunately, it sometimes has become the banner of overemphasizing *what* is right and wrong in social dilemmas while deemphasizing *how* Jesus navigated them. I've heard it used as an excuse to bypass the goal of relationship all together because "everyone just needs to know what is right and wrong." I've heard it being used as a free pass to fight back and retaliate because we need to defend God.

Really, is that necessary? Defend God?

I believe that God's all grown up, and he can handle himself. We don't ever see Jesus defending himself or the Father in this way.

I believe that God's all grown up, and he can handle himself.

I realize that not everyone in the family is misusing this phrase, but this is what I've experienced more often than not. It's a really important phrase that the family needs to get right. After all, the Holy Spirit, through Jude, is appealing to us to contend for the faith!

Remember, this issue is reaching a level of urgency that took precedence over discussing salvation more thoroughly. We see that this entire book was written to explain to the family what it looks like to contend for the faith. This is fabulous news! The family can be equipped to do this in the way of Jesus.

For Jude's audience, the issue that caused disunity was subtle and deceptive, and it went unnoticed. The issue wasn't blared through a megaphone of divisiveness; it's more like some people were one or two degrees off from the direction that everyone else was heading. At first, it didn't seem like much, but over time, the chasm grew. Jude wanted to give more details about who these people were, what they were doing, so that he could guide the church on contending for the faith. At this point in time, the largest wayward group he would be referring to were called the Libertines. Do you hear the word *liberty* in there? The Libertines believed that if this whole Jesus thing was about grace, then they should go ahead and be free, be unrestrained, give in to all sensuality. Basically, they were asking, "Why should we deny anything that we feel or that we want? We're covered by grace, so it can all be forgiven, right?"

This mentality is not far off from what I often heard as a professor. It sounded something like this: "Dr. Bryant, if I'm forgiven anyway, then why don't I just have a little fun right now? When I get close to death, which I'm sure is a long way off, I'll just repent really quick and be all good, right?" Or it would sound like this: "God's love is unconditional, right? Which means there's nothing I could do that would make him love me more and there's nothing I could do that would make him love me less. So, I'm just going to have fun for a little bit and then tap into that unconditional love later."

It's a legitimate question of many Christians today, and it was a foundational question for this rogue, Libertine sect of the early church. Here's what I've said those college students:

> Oh, you're right. I mean, you had the thief on the cross who got forgiven in the last moments of his life, and God is so good like that. However, faith is not just about forgiveness of sins or how much God loves you. Faith is a full, ongoing, growing relationship with God. You see, when you give your life to Christ you have access to what Jesus calls *living water*. God's love is like Niagara Falls, always flowing and so powerful. You have access to it through the Holy Spirit right away when you say yes to Jesus. When you give your life to Christ, it's like God gives you a cup, and because you're really thirsty, it's so refreshing to get a cup full of water from the waterfall. The longer you walk with Christ, the more relationship you build. Over time, it's like your cup gets replaced with a bucket, and then you get a wheelbarrow, and then you get a truck to get even more water. In fact, the more you grow in relationship with God, you're getting so much water that it's spilling out, and you can help refresh other people with the water that God's given you. In this ongoing, sanctifying relationship with God, **it's not that his love for you increases, it's that your ability to receive his love increases.** So it's way better to choose Christ now and start building

that relationship. Start getting filled up so you can pour out his love onto others. That's where full life is! **You can't pour out what you're not filled up with,** so choose now to follow his way.

Whether it's people today or the Libertines of the past, choosing to live with unrestrained sensuality and assuming it is just covered by grace is a strong temptation. Jude is concerned about the division this is causing in the family. He wants to guide the family to Jesus's method. No matter how upset someone may be or how wrong someone else is, there is a right way to engage our social dilemmas.

But there's more.

A different divisive thread of belief was also threatening to divide the family. Just like the Israelite spies who trusted their own negative experience of the promised land to determine their truth, there was a part of the family promoting experience-based truth. This way of thinking is gnosticism. In case you don't know what gnosticism is, let me give a quick intro because it certainly shows up in today's culture, just by different names. Gnosticism says that higher knowledge, the divine, or salvation is already in you, but it's been covered up with all kinds of hurts, mistakes, and so on. The truth is in you; it's only hidden. So if you can focus more on yourself, your personal experiences, self-discovery, and self-awareness, you'll find the source of truth. If you can peel back the layers you've built, you can discover your true self, and that's the way to the divine and to salvation. This comes up a lot in pop culture today, especially areas influenced by New Age spirituality. All you need to do is get rid of ignorance, decipher the patterns that weave through all of your experiences, and you will discover your true self. Basically, fully understanding my personal experiences and how I am wired will guide me to truth.

It can also sound like this: "If I just know myself better, I'll know God better. I can't know God unless I really know myself, who I really am." That's the sequence. As a psychologist by training, I believe that knowing yourself is a really good idea. God wired you in specific ways, and it's awesome. You are fearfully and wonderfully made (Ps. 139:14)! The problem with all this gnostic thinking is that the sequence of thought is backwards. Gnosticism promotes focusing on your own experiences to discover the truth of who you really are and the good things and the bad things about how you operate. You do this self-discovery first so that you can connect with God and love him the best way possible. Here's the problem with that: It's backwards. We're supposed to seek God first to then discover more about ourselves.

This sequencing problem goes all the way back to the garden of Eden, in a story that many of us are familiar with involving two trees. There was the Tree of Life and the Tree of the Knowledge of Good and Evil. There were not good and bad things on that second tree; the whole tree was death. This story is all about who we trust, who we will rely and depend on, God or myself. At the end of the day, we ask ourselves, "Am I fully trusting God?" If I am trusting God, I am receiving truth from him and that truth will influence my experience. In contrast, if I am trusting myself, I'm going to put everything I've got into studying my personal experiences. I'll look to break any ignorance I have by looking for patterns that seem to yield good results. I will make sure to repeat those "good" things and not repeat the patterns that lead to "bad" results. I will become so knowledgeable of the good things and bad things in my life, so self-aware in my experience, that it will lead me to truth. Once I achieve that, I will be like God. Ultimately, this tree declares that my experience is what gives me the truth about good and evil.

That's the choice: Tree of the Knowledge of Good and Evil, where my experiences create what is true, or Tree of Life, where God's truth influences my experiences.

> Ultimately, this tree declares that my experience is what gives me the truth about good and evil.

We see the gnostic fallacy play out with Adam and Eve and these two trees (Genesis 3). Eve had already received truth from God through Adam about what to do with these trees. However, look at how the serpent tempted her. He invited her to trust her experience over God's truth. She saw how beautiful the fruit looked, and she concluded truth from her experience. It would make her so wise. She would be like God. God's truth was no longer influencing her experience; her experience was now creating her truth. Do you see it? It's deceptive and subtle, isn't it? This is some of the same deception that Jude was concerned about in the church. It's not new to humanity; Satan just disguises it differently in different generations. This trick has been around for a long time, and unfortunately, people keep falling for it!

At this point, I often get this reaction: *Ted, I get it. But experiences seem so concrete, so trustworthy, so undeniable, so much like proof. I can feel my experience, I can see my experience, and it's got to be true because I'm discovering so much about myself and it's all making sense.*

It's not our experience that's the problem; it's the role we allow our experience to play. Our experience was never meant to bring us to truth about who we really are. We are supposed to first receive truth from God about who we are, and then that truth affects our experiences. Ultimately, if we let experiences determine truth, we are declaring that truth is already inside of us. We are capable of discovering it if we analyze things correctly, and now we've made the full circle back to gnosticism.

Do you see how gnostic thinking is so incredibly different than Christianity? So radically different than truth being a person, Jesus Christ, who we can do nothing on our own to have relationship with because of sin? Yet, through what Jesus did on the cross, right relationship with God is available now and forever. All truth comes from him, not us or our own experience. It's our relationship with Jesus that actually allows us to discover more of who we are made to be. Identity starts with who God says we are. Identity is a God right, not a human right. He created us; we did not create ourselves. God gets the right of telling us who we are. He is the source of all truth. It's the Holy Spirit inside of us that allows a direct connection to God. Over and over in scripture, God tests those in the family with this idea of experience-based truth. It's like he's saying,

> Hey, Ted, where are you at here? I know the truth you think your experience is showing you, but I'm calling you to something else beyond your understanding. My ways are beyond your ways (Isa. 55:9). A relationship with me as master, Lord, and sovereign over every experience is where you receive truth, and then that influences how you see your experiences. Do you trust me in that? Or do you have to understand everything? It's a heart dilemma, Ted. Do you want my truth, or do you want to create your own? You get to choose the tree to eat from, but it will come with consequences. That's not a threat Ted; that's reality.

Truth is not about self-discovery. Truth is about God-discovery. It's not about self-awareness. It's about Spirit awareness. These are very different things, and the lie of experience-based truth is so incredibly subtle. It worked its way into the garden of Eden, and Jude saw this lie work its way into the early church. Unfortunately, this same lie is alive and well in today's culture too, and is a real threat to the modern-day church. It seems that Jude wanted us to be aware of this lie and the social dilemmas surrounding it as a part of contending for the faith. Let's hold onto that realization as we continue.

Whether it is because of sensuality or self-discovery, division was happening in the early church. Jude saw disunity threatening the family. The consequences of this disunity are not new, and we can see similar ones today. Fracturing in the family can produce a tragic lack of belief that God is who he says he is. In addition, we see the direct impact of the two false belief systems we just discussed: lust and a desire for selfish gain. What would it be like to be our own gods? Doing what we want, when we want, how we want! To be just like God! *Sound familiar? Remember the two trees in the garden of Eden?*

As Jude is reminding us of these offenses, he had an insight about the Jesus Method. In each of these offenses, he referenced consequences that the Israelites would have been very familiar with, but with an important emphasis. In each of the accounts, Jude highlighted that God dealt out the discipline. He avenged the injustice. It's not humanity's role. People are not dealing out the consequences for unbelief. God is the only one who should be dishing out justice, and he does this in both the spiritual and physical realms. I believe there is so much repetition on this point that Jude is asking us, "Do you get it?" In the kingdom of God, retaliation has never been the role of humanity. That's God's job, according to his will. Jude was making it crystal clear. Humanity was always meant to do what Jesus did in social dilemmas: leave it up to the one who judges justly (1 Pet. 2:23).

This conclusion is an important emphasis in understanding the meaning of "contending for the faith," so let's lock it in.

Though the family is supposed to leave retaliation up to God in social dilemmas, it doesn't mean we should gloss over the danger that is sometimes present in guests. Jude illustrated this with a myriad of analogies to the dangerous deception that was occurring in the church. He was relentless in describing the horrific circumstances that the church found itself in with these offenders. All of his examples are juxtaposed to Jesus's own teaching and example. Jesus is the good shepherd (Ezek. 34:1–16); Bread of life (John 6:35); Living Water (John 7:37–39); sovereign over wind (Matt. 8:26); producer of the fruit of the Spirit (Gal. 5:22–23); and the way, truth, and life (John 14:6). Jude was trying to make it as clear as possible that these misaligned individuals were deceivers who had come to steal, kill, and destroy (John 10:10). Simultaneously, Jude also reminded us that God has already set aside punishment for them, so we do not need to be issuing discipline ourselves.

I think this balancing of awareness of evil while reserving judgment to God is one of the most challenging things about the Jesus Method. Jude explicitly reminded the family of the necessity of this balancing. Yes, complete ungodliness was happening, and the family was to leave retribution up to God.

Jude made it clear that these individuals had made up their heart and mind. They were ungodly in every way. They weren't interested in relationship with God, which means, according to the Jesus Method, we should respect their choice, walk away, and let God deal with them. This is what God has done over and over again throughout his story. Some people call that history, but I like *his*tory better!

Remember, this is all part of Jude's explanation of what contending for the faith means.

Understanding that God's got the punishment thing taken care of allows us to eventually walk away and leave the ungodly for God to deal with. These individuals Jude was talking about were full of unbelief, lust, and selfish gain, which was a full-on attack on the way of Jesus and everyone in the family. In fact, the words used to describe these individuals, *grumblers* and *malcontents*, would have taken the audience back to the wilderness in the book of Exodus. There, people grumbled about food and were malcontent about leaving Egypt. Their experience was driving their truth about the character of Moses and God himself. Jude set up a parallel situation here, and that generation in the wilderness all passed away, never reaching the promised land. *Who decided that?* God. Moses didn't issue that consequence. God did. *Can Jude be any more clear?* People are not supposed to retaliate; that's God's job!

> *Understanding that God's got the punishment thing taken care of allows us to eventually walk away and leave the ungodly for God to deal with.*

It may seem like Jude was belaboring the point about letting God be the judge, but clearly, he had seen enough of humanity to realize the vulnerability we have to playing God's role of judge. I believe that not much has changed today. If the family doesn't get this right, it's impossible for Jesus's social dilemma process to be fulfilled. There is only room for one judge in the Jesus Method, and it's not us.

This entire book sets up how bad the situation is in the church and how horrific these deceivers are. Jude was absolutely furious at what these guests were doing to the family. They were blaspheming God, trying to divide the family of God. They were trying to trick people into forming truth from their experiences and desires, just like the enemy did with Adam and Eve. This is not good, and he didn't want to talk about it, but he couldn't help it because it was so dangerous.

Have you felt that way before?

Perhaps there's something going on in your family, marriage, school, workplace, or online, and it's making you furious. You didn't really want to talk about it or address it, but it's gone too far at this point, and it's become too dangerous for you to stay silent. You feel like you should do something, but you're not sure exactly what to do. You might feel stuck or, honestly, you may be ready to go off on somebody! Before that happens, let's look at what the Holy Spirit through Jude lays out for the family to do in situations like this.

Like we have all felt at some point, Jude was deeply troubled by the social dilemma he was facing, so he must clearly lay out what the response of the family would be, what contending for the faith looks like with these deceiving guests who were hurting and dividing the family.

Ready for it?

Will it line up with our current Christian culture?

Will it align with what's in my own heart?

What are the marching orders of contending for the faith?

Let's find out:

> But you, beloved, building yourselves up in your most holy faith and praying in the Holy Spirit, keep yourselves in the love of God, waiting for the mercy of our Lord Jesus Christ that leads to eternal life. And have mercy on those who doubt; save others by snatching them out of the fire; to others show mercy with fear, hating even the garment stained by the flesh. (Jude 1:20–23)

WHAT?

WAIT!

No retaliation? Nothing.

No fighting back? Nope.

What about not backing down? We've already covered that one.

We must defend God, though, right? We've covered that one too.

Contending for the faith, according to Jude, is exactly what we would expect from the Jesus Method. The goal is always relationship—one relationship at a time through providing for guests' needs and then respecting the choices they make regarding faith. If they refuse relationship with God, then walk away and leave them to God. He is the one who will enact justice according to his will. And as family, we are always seeking to do the will of the Father. Jude was challenging the family to do this, and he was empowering them to pray in the Holy Spirit and remain in God's love.

Jude was imploring the family to build their own relationship with God through connection with the Spirit. In the face of angry, blaspheming, defiling guests, the family's number one priority is to keep themselves in the love of God. Focus on our relationship with God, asking him to refine us to have the most holy faith.

Incredible. Absolutely incredible!

There is not a single ounce of retaliation, argument, debate, or fight. For the family, there is no element of retribution, vengeance, or reckoning in Jude's instruction to contend for the faith. Simply increase your commitment to abide in God and trust the promises of Jesus (John 15).

I hope you can see that Jude's instruction on how the family should contend for the faith has very little to do with the people attacking them. Instead, it's about our own walk with Christ and making sure we are doing four things: building, praying, keeping, and waiting. We are to build our relationship with Jesus, be sensitive to the Holy Spirit in our prayers, keep listening to and obeying God, and wait for the mercy of God in our lives. This is what it means to contend for the faith, nothing more and nothing less. As we contend for the faith in this way, we will remain in the love of God, even when everyone else hates us or hates God.

Let's pause and ask, *How is this challenging me?* Take a moment to assess your heart and mind. What's your current blood pressure or heart rate?

Focusing first on my own relationship with God is a profound priority in contending for the faith. The first time I read through the book of Jude, it's not what I expected or, honestly, even what I wanted to hear, because everything inside of me naturally wants to fight back, to attack, or at least to defend. Everything in me wants to say to God, "What they're doing is not right. They're lying to people, hurting people, and we're just supposed to stand back and watch? Are we just going to let them get away with it? No!"

> *Focusing first on my own relationship with God is a profound priority in contending for the faith.*

They're not getting away with it. What they are doing is not right, so we are going to let God deal with it. It's evil, and God is the avenger who will rightfully repay (Rom. 12:19). It's not our job to avenge evil, but we better not sit back and watch either. Jude told us what we should be doing instead, and it's even more challenging (Jude 1:22–23).

He commanded the family to not immediately kick out family members who are starting to believe the lies. We are to have mercy. They do not need criticism, they need encouragement; they do not need tearing down, they need a building up. Come alongside them, one relationship at a time, and have dialogue. But there's more.

The family's work involves staying focused on the goal of relationship. Some guests are heading toward that fire. Regardless of our own feelings, thoughts, and experiences, God's truth says that he came to save the world, not condemn it (John 3:17). So as we follow Christ, if there is any God-given opportunity to snatch them out, provide for them, introduce them to Jesus, and then invite them into a relationship with him, we are to do it! We probably won't feel like it, but feelings should never take precedence over obedience. These might be the very people who have hurt us in the past, and we are to show them mercy. Why? Because that is the way of Jesus, confirmed by the cross. There's not a single retaliatory act that is being advised by Jude. It's his version of "turn the other cheek" (Matt. 5:39) or "bless those who persecute you" (Rom. 12:14). God's grace is unimaginable, and his expectation of the family to show that same grace in social dilemmas is clear.

Jude was cautioning the family. Show mercy, but make sure you don't fall into the power of sin with which the other person is currently wrestling. Out of our fear of, awe for, and reverence of God as truth, don't start liking, accepting, tolerating, or agreeing with that sin.

Jude 1:23 is the motivation behind a familiar phrase that I have heard among the family: "Hate the sin, love the sinner." I get what people are trying to say with this phrase, but it's not what Jesus modeled as our first response. From the very first chapter of this book, we see a different model. If someone is coming at me and they are covered in sin, "stained by the flesh" (Jude 1:23), my first response should not be to hate the sin, love the sinner. My first response is to work on the sin in my own life. I must be making sure I'm built up in Christ, praying in the Spirit about any "logs" in my eyes, remaining in the love of God, and expectantly waiting for his mercy in my own life. Once that humility is established, I can enter the Jesus Method with prayer, following the steps Jesus modeled.

There's no violence. There's no defense. There's no battle formation or strategy of counterattacks. Contending for the faith is not two boxing contenders going at each other. Jude is clarifying that we are to contend for the faith in our own hearts. As we are connected to the Spirit, we listen and obey what he is putting on our hearts to reach those around us. Continual connection with the Holy Spirit is key so he can remind us of all truth.

We are to contend for the faith in our own hearts.

I want to say something about being reminded of truth. The Bible is the living Word of God, full of truth, and the Holy Spirit wants to remind you of truth all the time (John 14:26). However, he cannot remind you of something that you never minded in the first place. *Are you tracking with me?* If we aren't disciplined in growing our relationship with God through reading the scriptures, the Holy Spirit can't bring it to the front of our attention because it was never a part of our attention in the first place. If you're in the family, then you must be in the scriptures hanging out with God.

Jude pointed to a very different contending than what our natural instincts want to do. The way of Jesus in his method is vastly different than the way of the world. Two completely different goals. The way of the world says that contending is fighting with someone, but in the Jesus way, contending is all about fighting for someone. I'm going to fight *for* my relationship with God. I'm going to fight *for* other family members' and guests' relationships with God without falling into sin myself. However, as Jesus demonstrated in previous social dilemmas and as Jude cautioned us, we must offer a holy respect if guests do not choose the way of Jesus. We are to provide for them and invite them, but we can't choose it for them. If they don't want it, we need to choose to walk away.

> *The way of the world says that contending is fighting with*
> *someone, but in the Jesus way, contending is all about fighting*
> *for someone.*

What an incredible book! Some of us are surprised, like I was, at the clarity with which Jude instructed the family to contend for the faith. It's not the fight with others that we often think it is. It's not the powering up of a theological stance or a resistant heart posture that we may *want* to have in certain moments. It's focused on relationship with an eternal perspective of God's sovereignty. Let's add it to the Jesus Method.

THE **JESUS** METHOD

STEP 1 Prayer

STEP 2A If family, then challenge and empower

STEP 2B If guest, then provide and respect

**If you are unsure as to whether they are family or guest, treat them as a guest.

Goal—Relationship with God and others

Pace—One relationship at a time

Strategy—Being a witness

Temptation—Experience creating truth

Perspective—God is in charge of the consequences for people's spiritual choices

Prayer

God, I know you have challenged me so many times about my natural instinct. My natural flesh wants to defend you. You're my friend—my best friend. You're my Savior, my Lord, and my God. I want to defend you, yet I don't see that in scripture. Jesus, I don't see you publicly defending yourself, and the only thing you've called us to defend is the hope that we have in you. God, I pray that you continue to work on me to be more like Jesus—to have deeper and richer relationship with you. You are truth, and I want to receive from you. I want to re-present you, not just what you said but how you did it—how you grew relationship. Lord, I pray that you continue to challenge any beliefs I've had about what weakness means or what passivity actually is. Help me to contend for the faith by wholeheartedly listening to and obeying you and then trusting that you will handle the consequences. I love you and trust you. In Jesus's name I pray, amen.

Prayerful Reflection

1. What are you feeling right now?
2. Are there any new insights or questions that you have about the Jesus Method?
3. How has your understanding of "contending for the faith" changed?
4. What is challenging you in this chapter?
5. What's your next step in contending for the faith in your own life?
6. What specific relationship does God want you to pray about?

CHAPTER 6

APPLYING THE METHOD

We have been able to establish the Jesus Method as we've been a witness to how he navigated social dilemmas. We also learned what "contending for the faith" means for family members, including a reminder that God is the one who wants to handle the consequences for people's spiritual decisions. Regardless of the circumstances that family members find themselves in, they can have confidence and peace about simply engaging the method that Jesus has laid out for us.

Jesus engaged in many other situations that corroborate his method. You might be familiar with some of these, and others you might not. As we review more examples, let's allow God to continue to transform our hearts so that we might be able to have more relationship with him. As we increase our clarity in the Jesus Method, it will increase our ability to apply it to our own lives. More repetitions equals further understanding, and further understanding equals greater application. We are going to go through the method, step by step, adding a wider variety of examples for each component.

Of course, many of these social dilemma situations could relate to more than one portion of the method, so I will emphasize the most pertinent contribution.

Step 1

Prayer

We have already talked about Jesus's prayer in John 17, but as a spiritual leader, he was constantly in conversation with and dependent on his heavenly Father while also in conversation with people in the physical realm, which we know from John 5:19. In addition, we also see Jesus letting his followers know how critical prayer is in social dilemmas. He prayed before choosing his twelve disciples (Luke 6:12), after John the Baptist was killed (Matt. 14:13), during the transfiguration (Matt. 17:1–13), while raising Lazarus from the dead (John 11:38–44), at the last supper (Matt. 26:17–30), walking to the garden of Gethsemane (John 15–17), in the garden itself (Matt. 26:36–45), and even while he was on the cross (Mark 15:34). Clearly, prayer is not the last resort of the Jesus Method. It's also not a "I guess I'll pray because nothing else is working" sort of mentality. That's not the way of Jesus. Prayer is the first priority and the foundation for social dilemmas.

When you think about the foundation of a building, it's impossible to build anything else until the foundation is set. You can't rush pouring the foundation; it takes time to have its full strength. It's the same with prayer. Think about a current social dilemma you are in, and spend some time in prayer about it right now. This is step 1 of the Jesus Method, and we shouldn't rush through it. I know sometimes we can be tempted to think we don't have time to pray, but we don't have time *not* to pray. Jesus models prayer as absolutely critical in his method. No matter the circumstance, Jesus took time to dialogue with God as he entered his social dilemmas.

Step 2

Family Time or Be Our Guest

Jesus was brilliant in how he navigated step 2 of his method. As we will see in these examples, Jesus engaged the guests and family members differently but always with the goal of more relationship. I love how God is so committed to this method that he starts it with Jesus's earthly parents. You never know how much impact their own witness of what God took them through made on Jesus as he was growing up. I can just imagine little Jesus saying, "Tell me the story again, Daddy, about the angel that came in your dream." God certainly challenged both Mary and Joseph from the beginning of Jesus's life. They were family, but that doesn't mean they were exempt from difficulty or pain. Difficulty is part of God's rhythm. Being in the family meant that they had access to the guidance and empowerment of God through that difficulty and pain. They endured staying together amid the social dilemma of outside pressure to divorce, traveling while uncomfortably pregnant only to give birth in a stable, and then uprooting suddenly and moving to Egypt. There were incredible challenges that God gave them, and he always was empowering them to succeed as they grew in their dependence on him (Luke 1–2; Matthew 1–2). All that they had to sacrifice for God and for each other during the pregnancy (reputation, convenience, TEAM) only grew their SQ for God, each other, and Jesus. With the family, God is always more interested in preparation than he is comfort. Steps always can be taken into further relationship if we are willing to make that sacred choice.

> With the family, God is always more interested in preparation than he is comfort.

Jesus grew up and had the opportunity to reveal himself as fulfilling the prophecy of Isaiah in his hometown of Nazareth. This is a social dilemma because it would be perceived as blasphemous, and we already know the consequence of that one. It's death. We see in Luke 4 that sure enough, all the people in the synagogue tried to kill him. According to the Jesus Method, he can see that they were choosing to become guests at that point, so he respected their decision and walked away from them.

In another social dilemma, Jesus was met by a man with leprosy (Luke 5). According to the law, lepers were to be avoided at all costs so others didn't become unclean in the eyes of God. Jesus had a guest in front of him, so Jesus provided what the man needed and healed him by touching him. Jesus challenged the man, now part of the family, to go show himself to the priests and offer the sacrifices that Moses commanded as a testimony to them. The judgments the world had made on the leper did not stop Jesus from providing for him. The same must be true for the family today. Is there any guest in your life for whom you have not provided because of how they are viewed in society? Following the way of Jesus in our social dilemmas is going to cost our comfort and convenience, but that is what relationship requires.

Once a paralyzed man was lowered through the roof of a crowded house in which Jesus was teaching (Luke 5; Matthew 9). This man was a guest in the house literally and spiritually! Jesus provided for his spiritual needs by forgiving his sins and then provided for his physical needs by healing his body. Jesus sent the man home, and the man left praising God as a powerful witness. God is big enough to work on everyone in every situation. At the same time Jesus was providing for a guest, he also was challenging those who claim to be a part of the family. He invited the Pharisees into a relationship with him by choosing to believe that he was who he said he is: the Son of Man. They refused in their hearts and thus showed themselves to be guests. As a result, Jesus respected their decision and walked away.

God is big enough to work on everyone in every situation.

The Pharisees came back to Jesus later and tried to trap him by asking him a question about paying taxes (Matthew 22; Luke 20). Jesus challenged them greatly with his answer about giving back to Caesar what is Caesar's but giving God what is God's. Jesus was referring to all of who we are (SQ, TEAM) because we bear the image of God, just like the coin bore the image of Caesar. Seeking power once again, it is recorded that the Pharisees were doing this in a public space (Luke 20:26). Notice that Jesus did not shy away from his method, even in the face of engaging money and politics. No topic was outside of his method.

Jesus had his hands full with his own disciples. One day he sent them ahead into a Samaritan village to prepare some things for him, but the villagers rejected them. Immediately, we read this in Luke 9:54: "When the disciples James and John saw this, they asked, 'Lord, do you want us to call fire down from heaven to destroy them?'" A couple of things here. Their response to the rejection of these Samaritans (guests) was to have a show of power; clearly, their hearts were not aligned with Jesus. His method was to respect the faith choices of the guest and to make it personal, not public. Jesus challenged his disciples by rebuking their desire for retaliation and then instructed them to move on to the next village. At times some of our most challenging dilemmas are within our closest relationships.

These are difficult because there often are intense emotions based on the history of the relationship. Even so, Jesus modeled journeying through his method in these situations as well.

One of my favorite social dilemmas that Jesus entered was with another expert in the law (Luke 10). The expert asked Jesus a similar question to the rich, young ruler: "What must I do to inherit eternal life?" However, we know that this man was testing Jesus (Luke 10:25). The expert had a heart dilemma. After Jesus responded to him correctly, the man asked one more question to justify himself. Note the parallelism that exists between this story and that of the rich, young ruler. This man wanted to make sure he was doing all the right things in life. He thought that the goal was doing a bunch of right things and staying away from wrong things. He was living with an overemphasis on the *what*. The man needed to know who exactly he should be loving.

Jesus knew that the goal of relationship was more important than the rights and wrongs that we do. It was time to challenge another person claiming to be in the family. Jesus told the story of the Good Samaritan. In this story, the religious professionals followed their rights and wrongs about an unclean individual on the side of the road, but a "despised" Samaritan showed mercy on the man who had been beaten up and left for dead. He provided for all his needs in that moment and in the near future. Why? This is what loving relationship requires. The Samaritan demonstrated a high SQ by giving up his TEAM to care for this man. Wherever our TEAM goes, relationship grows. Jesus was laying it on thick here. To answer the expert in the Law's question, the Samaritan, who the expert would have greatly disliked, was the hero who demonstrated how to love your neighbor. Then Jesus said, "Go and do likewise" (Luke 10:37), empowering the expert with his next step in relationship with God if he chose it.

Guests and family alike can be tempted to get caught up in justifying themselves, like the expert in this story. Jesus reinforces that we must stay focused on relationship, not reputation. When we lock in on building Christ-centered relationships, reputation will follow in time. When we follow the Jesus Method, our worldly reputations will take a hit as we provide instead of overpower, invite instead of instigate. Jesus continued to exemplify this when he was traveling through Samaria.

Going through Samaria was a wrong thing to do, according to Jewish customs. During his journey he did another wrong thing by stopping to talk to a Samaritan woman at a well. We learn quickly in the story that she was a guest who had sinned many times over with sexual immorality. Following his method, he provided for her needs, which were spiritual in nature this time, and he invited her into a relationship with him that would save her life. She said yes, became part of the family, and then ran to be a witness in her village. Running back to her village was her own social dilemma because it was full of people who despised her. What was her strategy for handling all of that? She was a witness to what God has done for her. The disciples were seriously challenged because it went against lingering values they had about prioritizing right and wrong behavior over relationship. It's an incredible story, and I invite you to go read the full thing right now (John 4) to see every step of the Jesus Method come to life.

Jesus told a beautiful parable about a family in the middle of a social dilemma (Luke 15). God is cast as the Father figure, and he has two sons in the story. The younger one was clearly a guest due to him asking for his father's inheritance. Basically, the younger son said, "The only thing that is valuable about you, Dad, is what you can give me when you're gone. How about we pretend that you're dead and you give it to me right now?" How did the father respond?

He respected the choice that the younger son made and let him leave with his inheritance. So far so good with the Jesus Method. Then the younger son hit rock bottom, chose to humble himself, and tried to have relationship again with his father. The goal of God is always relationship, and the father welcomed him back with open arms and celebrated him as part of the family. Some of us have lived like this prodigal son, and God has welcomed us into the family. We know what it is like to move from ashamed to celebrated, all because of God's grace. He wants us to be a witness to what he has done. God wants to use us to carry his invitation to other prodigals who are lost and alone.

However, there's more.

The older son, who had always claimed to be a part of the family, was angry about what his father just did, and he refused to join the celebration. His heart clearly did not want restored relationship. He believed that right behavior should earn salvation and celebration, not relationship. The older son's entire defense and justification to his dad was about him being the son who did all the right things in his life and not messing up like his younger brother. Listen to how committed the father is to relationship, though: "'My son,' the father said, 'you are always with me, and everything I have is yours. But we had to celebrate and be glad, because this brother of yours was dead and is alive again; he was lost and is found'" (Luke 15:31–32). The father said nothing about right and wrong behavior in challenging the older son's heart. He simply went to the higher goal of relationship, pointing out the opportunity that the older son always had for oneness with the father. This sounds like Jesus's prayer in John 17 again! In contrast, the younger son didn't have this opportunity because he was "dead" and "lost," but now he did, so the relationship that the younger son finally wanted must be celebrated. Remember, that's the goal. We don't know how the older son reacted to this challenge. That's where the parable ends. Once again, we see Jesus challenging someone claiming to be family and empowering him to celebrate another step in relationship. At the same time, Jesus provided for the guest—the younger brother—in hopes that he would choose relationship and be a part of the family, which he did.

As we witnessed in the prodigal son story, Jesus is equally committed to both guests and family. I am amazed by this because we as humans usually seem to prefer one over the other. As we look at our current relationships, we likely will find more of a passion for either guests or family members. Though I do not think the quantity of these different individuals needs to be equal, I do believe Jesus models a strong pursuit of whomever God places in front of us. Regardless of whether God provides guests or family in our impact circles, we are to follow through on the Jesus Method with all that we've got.

Another example of Jesus providing for guests shows up in his first miracle (John 2). A wedding is in need of more wine, and Jesus did not get into a big debate about it. Though he did challenge his mother a bit, he simply provided for a need. The result? We're not exactly sure who all decided to form relationship with God because of it; however, we do know that there were several opportunities for relationships to grow. For example, relationships could have grown between the servants helping with the wedding and Jesus as well as among the disciples and Jesus, and the newlyweds now had more substantial relationships with those who came to the wedding.

In John 3, Jesus challenged Nicodemus, who claimed to be in the family. Jesus invited Nicodemus to start a new relationship with God through Jesus. Jesus then empowered him with how to do it: be "born again." One of the things I love about this encounter is that Nicodemus's heart was in a dilemma. He was earnestly trying to understand the way and method of Jesus, but he didn't get it yet. However, as we track Nicodemus's story throughout the rest of the Gospels, we see him eventually choose to be a part of God's family. His new relationship with God was marked by sacrificing his reputation to help bury the body of Jesus, which shows a high SQ (John 19:38–42).

One of the most powerful family challenge moments I see in the Gospels is when Jesus said that people need to "eat the flesh of the Son of Man and drink his blood" (John 6:53 NIV). I can just imagine the response of everyone there listening to him: "Um, what did he just say? We need to eat his body and drink his blood? OK, I'm good with all the healings and stuff, but I can't do that. I'm out." Sure enough, many of his followers left that day, and Jesus point-blank asked his twelve disciples, "You do not want to leave too, do you?" (John 6:67 NIV). Jesus was challenging them hard right there, but he was also inviting them into deeper relationship. How? Listen to the way Simon Peter responded: "We have come to believe and to know that you are the Holy One of God" (John 6:69 NIV). They refused to let the temptation of their experience determine their truth. They were committed to believing beyond their understanding, except for one, Judas, who Jesus already knew would betray him (John 6:70). Judas refused to accept the relationship that Jesus had for him. What did Jesus do? He respected the spiritual choice that Judas made, and Jesus did not try to stop him. I can't imagine how hard that must have been for Jesus! God the Father was challenging Jesus, too, into deeper relationship and oneness with him. God is always more interested in the family's preparation than their comfort. We can expect similar difficulties in our own lives. He will comfort along the way, but it's while we are being challenged and empowered to grow in relationship.

Goal

Relationship with God and Others

We have already seen that Jesus's goal in his method is always relationship. Some other great moments in the life and ministry of Jesus further substantiate this. For example, Jesus invited Levi, also known as Matthew, to leave behind his tax collector job and be in relationship with Jesus as one of his twelve disciples. First, this had to seem like a crazy decision to everyone, including the religious leaders and Jesus's own disciples. By being a tax collector, Matthew would have broken the Law of Moses many times. He would not have been liked by anyone and would have been known as a big-time sinner to the whole city. This is why the religious leaders were so disgusted when they saw Jesus going over to Matthew's house to have dinner with all of his sinner friends (Luke 5). The goal of the Pharisees and Sadducees was to maintain the right and wrong of the law. They had a singular focus on the *what* of God's law. If someone was doing something wrong compared to the Law, then it was wrong. No exceptions! They certainly would not try to form relationship.

We see a parallel situation with Jesus going over to the house of Zacchaeus, another tax collector (Mark 19). In both of these social dilemmas, Jesus undeniably placed opportunity for relationship over right or wrong behavior. He provided for their emotional and psychological needs of being chosen, honored, and included in relationship with others. After providing for them, Jesus invited them into the family. The sinners say yes. Jesus won, and he got to have relationship with them as a part of the family. Can you feel the vibe of the closing scene of the prodigal son story all over again? Jesus kept hammering it home. Restored relationship trumps everything.

He provided for their needs, invited them into the family, and then respected whatever choice was made. He's happier if the choice is yes, but he will respect it either way.

Regardless of how the family may view certain guests or how guests may view the family, Jesus engages his method head-on with whoever God places in front of him. Relationship is what is driving Jesus, and it should be what constantly drives us as well. It doesn't matter how the rest of the world deciphers our attempts to grow relationship. We can leave those consequences up to God.

Another set of in-the-face social dilemmas that Jesus had with the Pharisees happened on the Sabbath. The Law of Moses held the Sabbath day as holy, and people were not supposed to do any work. However, the religious leaders had added many specific stipulations of what rest and work meant that went far beyond what God had intended. Jesus's disciples picking grain on the Sabbath because they were hungry is one of those examples (Matthew 12; Mark 2; Luke 6). Jesus also healed a man on the Sabbath (Matthew 12; Luke 6) while challenging the religious leaders about their hypocrisy of saving their own sheep on the Sabbath. He also healed a crippled woman on the Sabbath (Luke 13) and a crippled man on the Sabbath (John 5). In both cases, the religious leaders exhibited no celebration for the restoration of relationship that Jesus's healing brought. They were only indignant at the violation of the Law. The goal of Jesus in these social dilemmas is crystal clear: relationship. The goal of relationship is more important than making sure someone is doing all the right things and staying away from all the wrong things. Depending on how you grew up, that last statement may not sit well with you, but the truth of it is undeniable when you see Jesus's method. We need to remember that obedience to the way of Jesus is more important than our traditions, upbringings, or feelings.

There is another story of Jesus that highlights this priority of relationship but in a new way. Jesus was hanging out with two of his friends one day, and one of the friends was sitting with Jesus having conversation and building relationship, while the other was busy serving Jesus and any other friends who came into the house (Luke 10). These two sisters were in a dilemma. Now, if you already know this story, try to think about it with a fresh perspective. One woman chose to sit with Jesus (Mary), and one woman chose to serve Jesus and others (Martha). Both of these actions seemed like good things to do. Serving Jesus and serving other people are both a "right" thing to do. However, Jesus said that what Mary was doing— building relationship—was the better option. Growing relationship *with* God is still the highest goal, even when the other option is a lot of right stuff you could be doing for God.

Taking time to build relationship with God is never a waste of time. It's never the lesser option. God is saying that compared to relationship, it doesn't matter how busy we are doing "right" things. It's just not good if those things are distracting us from giving our best TEAM to God. That's what was happening to Martha in the story. If this is the routine or rat race you find your-self in right now in life, God doesn't want you to feel ashamed. These are just like the rumble strips on the road, reminding you that there is a better option. God misses you. He wants to hang out with you. That's more valuable to him than anything else you might be doing *for* him. Even if one of those things is reading this book, put it down and go take a walk with God. Spend some time with him and let him fill you with the peace that comes from his presence.

Taking time to build relationship with God is never a waste of time.

This conclusion is especially convicting for me in my own life. I often can be working hard serving people by doing things for them without taking the time to form relationship. There is a lot to do around the church, in my own house, in my neighborhood, on my kids' sports teams, and in surrounding community. In my mind, I *think* I'm doing the most good by accomplishing the most tasks. I say to myself that I'm being efficient and strategic. I'm optimizing my efforts by doing the most good for the most number of people. Unfortunately, the reality is that I often am missing opportunities to establish what is most important: relationship with God and others. More often than not, I need to be reminded to sit and be present with someone. As things need to get done, we can do them together instead of dividing and conquering.

Jesus continued to emphasize the goal of relationship when he was hanging out at Simon the leper's house one time. A woman walked in with a big jar of expensive perfume (Matthew 26; John 12). She then proceeded to pour it on Jesus's head, anointing him right then and there. *Was this a good thing to do?* In those days, sure, but the disciples were upset because they thought it would have been better to sell the perfume and use the money received to feed the poor. We have another dilemma of comparing two really good things: building relationship with Jesus through sacrificing something valuable (higher SQ), or feeding the poor, which would have been considered the more righteous act according to the Law. Again, both were good things, but Jesus challenged his disciples to understand that building relationship with God, especially through personal sacrifice (higher SQ), is always more important than doing righteous acts. It reminds me of what Jesus shared about the widow's offering compared to those who gave more in quantity: "They all gave out of their wealth; but she, out of her poverty, put in everything—all she had to live on" (Mark 12:44). It's not about the quantity of resources someone could give; it's about the willingness to sacrifice resources to further relationship with God. Higher levels of relationship require higher levels of sacrifice.

Jesus continued to prioritize relationship over right and wrong behaviors when he established the New Covenant at the last supper (Matt. 26:28; Mark 14:24; Luke 22:20). A promise based on relationship replaced a promise based on the Law of right and wrong. Relationship is the goal, and when people are in relationship with God, right action will flow out of them. Jesus sacrificed not to change people's behaviors, but to change their relationship with God. Relationship is that important, and it's why it's the goal of God and should be the goal of the family in every social dilemma.

> *Jesus sacrificed not to change people's behaviors, but to change their relationship with God.*

Pace

One Relationship at a Time

Not only was Jesus serious about the goal of every social dilemma being increased relationship with God and others, but there was a particular pace that he modeled. The pace is one relationship at a time, which, if I'm being honest, is way too slow for me! I often think to myself, *If the goal is relationship, then why not a ton of relationships at once?*

It doesn't work like that.

Dr. R. Mark Beeson, the founding pastor at our church, used to say all the time, "Velocity and intimacy are enemies." True relationships form the best at lower velocities and one at a time. When you are trying to connect with someone at high speed, that's a collision, not a connection. In that sort of relationship crash, you might be attached together, but there's going to be damage in that relationship that'll need to be repaired.

It's not a mistake that Jesus called each of his disciples by name as he invited them to follow him. Even as Jesus was going through the region healing everyone who needed it, look at how the pace is described: "Now while the sun was setting, all those who had any who were sick with various diseases brought them to Him; and He was laying His hands on each one of them and healing them" (John 4:40 NASB). Jesus was laying his hands on *each one* of them, one relationship at a time. Jesus had the power to heal them all in a moment, but that sort of efficiency wasn't the highest goal. His goal was relationship, and that required a pace of one at a time. *How convicting is that?* I know that in my life, I have often fallen victim to the lie that "just because I can, I should." The bigger, the better! We see Jesus blow up that lie over and over in his life. He was unwilling to cheapen relationship, knowing the best relationships form at a pace of one person at a time.

We see this again with the woman who was healed from twelve years of bleeding (Luke 8:43–48). The fact that she got healed was great, but Jesus stopped and turned to find her and look her in the eye, because he wanted relationship. He knew that she needed to feel chosen, seen, and accepted, so he maintained a pace of one relationship at a time. This healing happened when he was on his way to help an official (Jairus) whose daughter was sick (Luke 8:49–56; Matthew 9; Mark 5). When they got to the home, she had already passed away, but Jesus went into the house and, interestingly, kicked everyone out except the parents and a few of his disciples. This was a personal moment, not a public one, because Jesus wanted relationship. He had relationships to grow, one relationship at a time, and he was starting with one little girl who had fallen "asleep," as he called it. Sure, more people could have been impressed and amazed if he would have let them stay in the house to watch. However, being impressive with more people and wowing the crowd were not his goals—relationship was—and Jesus was fully committed to do whatever relationship requires.

It's amazing that we even see this pace show up in some of Jesus's parables. Jesus told three consecutive stories about a lost sheep, lost coin, and lost son (which we've already discussed) (Luke 15). What's fascinating about these stories is that they all uphold the value of one relationship at a time. The shepherd risked the whole flock for one lost sheep. A woman searched tirelessly for one lost coin, and the father saw his lost son coming from a long way off and ran to him. Just to make sure that the listeners got the importance of one relationship at a time, Jesus said, "In the same way, I tell you, there is rejoicing in the presence of the angels of God over one sinner who repents" (Luke 15:10).

I know that this pace of one relationship at a time could be frustrating for some of us because it seems too slow; however, it could also be relieving. I was speaking to a businesswoman on this topic one day after a weekend church service. She came up to me with a big smile on her face and expressed how relieved she was about the message that day. I asked her what in particular stood out to her. She shared that she always felt so much pressure to reach hundreds of people at her job with the gospel. Today, she realized that her pace could change to one person at a time, whatever that one person needed for relationship. She had always questioned if focusing on a smaller group of people was a big enough goal for her to strive for. God took that incredible pressure and weight off of her. She ended our conversation exclaiming that she was excited to go to work the next day, focused on one relationship at a time. She smiled and said, "I can do that!"

If you have ever felt a similar pressure, you can let it go. The only pressure we need to experience is the pressure to listen to and obey God. This is part of the fear of the Lord that we see repeatedly in scripture. It is a healthy pressure that keeps us in close relationship with God. In Jesus's method, obedience includes honoring the pace he modeled, one relationship at a time. We can do that!

Strategy

Being a Witness

Let's move into the strategy that is involved in the Jesus Method and how it is radically different from what we typically see in our world today. When it comes to social dilemmas, the strategy of the world involves gaining as much power as possible, which inevitably will bring about some intimidation or fear in the competition. Thus, the more power someone has, the more fear they can instill in others, which should result in more victories. We already saw this sort of pattern with Jesus's miraculous healing of the demon-possessed man. The townspeople assumed that Jesus must be dangerous since he had so much power. Jesus countered the world's strategy, not with a greater show of power but with a greater witness. Social dilemmas were not power struggles to Jesus; they were about relationship. It was by surrendering all his power on the cross that he enabled the opportunity for people to have right relationship with God. It was the joy of relationship that was before him that he endured the cross (Heb. 12:2).

His victory over death, hell, and the grave came through *giving up* his power. Jesus's strategy and the world's strategy go in opposite directions, so it's no surprise that we see them clash when Jesus was arrested (John 18). The guards showed up in full force, and as a natural, worldly response to all of that power, Peter drew his own sword and chopped off the ear of the servant of the high priest. Jesus's strategy was not about brute physical force; it was about being a witness to God's will at all costs. That's why when Peter did this,

"Jesus commanded Peter, 'Put your sword away! Shall I not drink the cup the Father has given me?'" (John 18:11). Over the next twenty-four hours of Jesus's life, the strategy of the world flexed its power through many people: the soldiers binding him up in the garden; the high priest, the high council, and guards spitting on Jesus, mocking him, and slapping him; Pilate threatening him; and the Roman guards doing the same things as the Jewish high council by dishonoring, mocking, and beating him, just with more brutality. Then there was the cross, the ultimate power play. The cross was the symbol of fear, power, and control across the Roman world. Even after Jesus was dead and buried in the tomb, the Roman and Jewish leaders continued to use the strategy of power. They posted powerful guards at the tomb to make sure nothing would happen. They thought this show of power was the way to make sure they had the final victory over this Jesus movement.

Throughout this whole sequence, God enabled the strategy of his will to be made known. Jesus was a witness to being the I AM at his arrest, and the soldiers fell back twice. Jesus was a witness to being the son of God to the high priest and high council as well as to Pilate. In fact, the witness of Jesus's identity was posted in three languages above his head on the cross. Jesus being a witness to God's sovereign will played itself out throughout those twenty-four hours. It certainly is not the easier strategy when faced with a volatile social dilemma. What Peter did with his sword was easier. Consider that he had no trouble drawing a sword to show power, but in the next few hours, he failed three times to be a witness of the relationship he had with Jesus. Though more difficult, being a witness is the most effective strategy. We see this on Easter morning, when Mary was tasked with being a witness to the greatest news ever. Over the course of the next few weeks, hundreds of people were eyewitnesses to the resurrected Jesus, and the strategy of Jesus became unstoppable!

Jesus tried to address this strategic difference several times with his followers. "Don't be like the rulers of this world," he told them in Mark 10:42–45, "who just lord their power over others." Instead, be a slave and a servant of others by serving them. What was Jesus's justification for this difference? Himself. He came not to be served but to serve (Matt. 20:28).

In one of his last times with all of his disciples, Jesus told them the secret to how the rest of the world would know that they were Jesus's disciples. It wasn't because they could cast out demons, heal the sick, or do other miraculous things. It wasn't by how they were going to power up politically and militarily to rally Israel against Rome. It wasn't even about how they might argue their theological stances in the court of law. It was by being a witness to the way Jesus loved them and by loving each other in the same way (John 13:34–35).

Before we roll into the next step of the Jesus Method, let's make sure we digest what Jesus established in his call to love others the way he had loved them. Jesus claimed that ultimate victory was not through a strategy of philosophy, power, or politics, but by being witnesses to how the disciples had been loved by Christ. Again, the family must take Jesus's strategy seriously. Do not let witness envy creep into your heart or mind, and remember that God will give you the words you need at the right time (Luke 12:12).

Temptations

Experience Creating Truth

One of the biggest temptations that we see in the Jesus Method is the temptation of forming truth from our experience instead of receiving truth directly from God. I want to walk through a few more examples of where this temptation appeared in Jesus's ministry.

It showed up right at the start! Jesus got baptized, and then the Holy Spirit took him out to the wilderness to be tempted by the devil (Matthew 4; Luke 4). Jesus obviously was in the family, so the heavenly Father challenged him, preparing him for what was ahead in ministry. As you read through the temptations from the devil and then Jesus's responses, a couple of things stand out. First, Jesus was being empowered to handle these temptations by believing in the truth of scripture. Second, these temptations were trying to get him to do just the opposite: let his experience determine his truth. *Come on, Jesus, you're hungry . . . like, literally starving. Don't you feel that? Your experience is the most concrete truth you have right now, Jesus. Just turn these stones to bread.* Jesus was tempted to let his experience of hunger determine what he should do next. In the second temptation it wasn't about Jesus's truth; it was about helping other people not let their experience determine their truth. *Come on, Jesus, you want them to believe in you, right? So just jump off this temple, and when they see you rescued by angels, they will believe that you are who you say you are.* Jesus was tempted to let other people determine their truth about him based on what they experiences. Notice that Jesus went straight to scripture first when rebuking each temptation. It's by the truth of scripture that he resisted these temptations. Finally, the third temptation brought him the opportunity to rule the world if he just bowed down to the devil. *Come on, Jesus, I know you want to rule. You want to have power. You're human, after all. There's not a more satisfying truth than worldly success and being able to have the power to get what you want, when you want it, and how you want it.* Jesus was tempted to let the experience of world power be his truth. Yet again, it is the truth he received through the scriptures that allowed him to rebuke the devil and have victory over this third temptation.

We also see this choice of where to receive truth show up several more times in the Gospels. One example is when Peter received truth from God instead of his own conclusions from experience. Jesus and his disciples were traveling in Caesarea Philippi: "He said to them, 'But who do you say that I am?' Simon Peter replied, 'You are the Christ, the Son of the living God.' And Jesus answered him, 'Blessed are you, Simon Bar-Jonah! For flesh and blood has not revealed this to you, but my Father who is in heaven'" (John 16:15–17).

Peter's truth came straight from God.

In contrast, a great example of people falling into this temptation of experience-based truth came from the religious leaders. They were talking with Jesus one day and demanding a miraculous sign from him (Mark 8:11). If they could only experience something godly, they would believe Jesus is of God. That's the wrong order, and Jesus didn't fall for it. He did not give them a sign, and he left. Later, when Jesus was hanging on the cross, the religious leaders and others passing by begged Jesus to let them experience a miracle so that they may believe truth about him. They said, "Let the Christ, the King of Israel, come down now from the cross that we may see and believe" (Mark 15:32). Once again, the way of the world desperately wanted proof in their experience to form truth. However, the way of Jesus receives truth from God first, which then affects experiences.

When we are thinking about our current social dilemmas how does this temptation of experience-based truth come into play? I have found that our negative experiences with people, organizations, or communities persuade us to respond with power in negative ways, further breaking relationship. It's our experience of hurt that leads us to believe that a critical response is best. Powering up becomes our experience-based truth, but Jesus shows us that surrendering power is surprisingly most effective. From my personal experience, this is an incredible challenge for the family to follow, and yet it is undeniably a part of the Jesus Method.

Perspective

God Is in Charge of the Consequences for People's Spiritual Choices

Social dilemmas with family members and guests alike can rile us up! When the emotions are gearing up and the sense of injustice is rising to the forefront of our minds, we must maintain Jesus's perspective on the situation. God is God, and I am not. There is only one judge and issuer of consequence and discipline for spiritual choices, and it's not me. One time when Jesus was surrounded by a crowd, including the religious leaders, he wanted them all to know that God oversees the consequences of people's spiritual choices. He told a parable about a master of a house, who represents the God character. The master planted a vineyard, leased it to tenants, and left to go to another country (Matt. 21:33–46; Mark 12; Luke 20). At harvest time, he sent back several rounds of servants to gather his portion, but each time they were beaten and killed by the tenants. So eventually, he sent his son, thinking that the tenants would surely respect his son, but they killed him as well. Jesus then asked the question to the audience: "'Therefore, when the owner of the vineyard comes, what will he do to those tenants?' 'He will bring those wretches to a wretched end,' they replied, 'and he will rent the vineyard to other tenants, who will give him his share of the crop at harvest time'" (Matt. 21:40–41 NIV). Is Jesus being clear enough? Notice that after the first round of servants being killed, successive servants who came were not supposed to fight the tenants—not even the son was supposed to fight back in any way—but God eventually would deal with them. The consequences of people's spiritual choices are God's to handle, no one else.

Later on in Jesus's ministry, he once again was clear about who is supposed to be doing the judging: "If anyone hears my words but does not keep them, I do not judge that person. For I did not come to judge the world, but to save the world. There is a judge for the one who rejects me and does not accept my words; the very words I have spoken will condemn them at the last day" (John 12:48 NIV). God is the judge, which means the gavel is not ours to carry. We must keep letting go of it when we are in social dilemmas.

As we close out this chapter on other portions of scripture that continue to substantiate the Jesus Method, what is God putting on your heart? I know that you've seen the questions at the end of every chapter, and in case you haven't engaged those yet, this might be a good time. Pause and pray, and then journey through them, trying to pay attention to what God is showing you. We never want to miss what God is trying to tell us.

Prayerful Reflection

1. What are any new insights that God is putting on your heart from this chapter?
2. What is God challenging you in right now?
3. What area of the Jesus Method do you resonate with the most? Why?
4. What part of the process are you wrestling with the most? Why?
5. What are other examples of Jesus's method that you can think of in scripture?
6. What relationship is God wanting you to pray for after reading this chapter?

CHAPTER 7

THE HOLY SPIRIT'S PROCESS

So far, we've journeyed through the vast majority of the social dilemmas that we see Jesus involved in. Based on the consistency with which we see Jesus navigating those, we have outlined the Jesus Method. One of the main reasons why people don't naturally engage this method is because of a desire to fight back in some way—attacking someone's stance or wanting to defend God as a retaliation of some sort. In fact, this might be assumed to be a good, strong response, especially considering our natural understanding of "contending for the faith." However, we learned from the Holy Spirit, through Jude, that contending for the faith does not involve retaliation or revenge of any sort. It is a focus on our own faith-filled relationship with God and on relationships that God has put around us. We are to trust in him to oversee the consequences for people's spiritual decisions. We are to remember that he's the judge, not us.

Beyond what we see in Jude, it would be helpful to continue to check the consistency of the Jesus Method as implemented by the Holy Spirit in the early church. The family has the same Spirit today, so if we continue to see him use the Jesus Method, it will corroborate even more that this is the process we are to engage in as well.

We talked about the importance of constantly reading through the Scriptures earlier so that the Holy Spirit can remind us of them. As you come through Revelation, you realize that it's not going to get any less messy before the end, and it's pretty messy right now. There are a lot of hurt people hurting people, and confused people confusing people. As loved people, God is calling the family to love people. We were born for the purpose of following God's will in such a time as this. So let's continue to lean in with an open mind and a humble heart, giving God permission to refine us in any way that he sees fit.

> *There are a lot of hurt people hurting people, and confused people confusing people. As loved people, God is calling the family to love people.*

Let's go to the book of Acts, where Jesus has gone back to heaven and he has sent the Holy Spirit to the family to help them spread the gospel across the world. By no means is this a comprehensive review of every social dilemma in the early church, but I do hope to show the Holy Spirit's continuity of the Jesus Method.

Here it is one more time.

THE **JESUS** METHOD

STEP 1 Prayer

STEP 2A If family, then challenge and empower

STEP 2B If guest, then provide and respect

**If you are unsure as to whether they are family or guest, treat them as a guest.

Goal—Relationship with God and others

Pace—One relationship at a time

Strategy—Being a witness

Temptation—Experience creating truth

Perspective—God is in charge of the consequences for people's spiritual choices

One of the first social dilemmas that we see in the early church happens in Acts 3:1–4a:

One day Peter and John were going up to the temple at the time of prayer—at three in the afternoon. Now a man who was lame from birth was being carried to the temple gate called Beautiful, where he was put every day to beg from those going into the temple courts. When he saw Peter and John about to enter, he asked them for money. Peter looked straight at him, as did John.

Already we see these disciples following in the footsteps of Jesus, directing their gaze in a loving way on this lame man. It reminds me of how Jesus looked on the rich, young ruler. Ever since I've studied some of the context of that gaze, I can't help but notice every time in scripture that Jesus or a disciple "looks upon someone." There's something sacred about eye-to-eye contact because a vulnerability is built into that moment, and it's hard to hide when you're locked in on someone. I have kids, and I've certainly experienced this. Those times when the kids refuse to make eye contact, it doesn't matter what's coming out of their mouths—they're hiding something! At the same time, have you ever tried to communicate something meaningful and loving to someone, but they won't look at you? You can't do it! Looking at each other is key to fully conveying your heart. In the social dilemmas of our lives, eye contact slows you down and allows you to see one person at a time. Moments like those have powerful relationship-building potential. That's why Peter and John wanted to have eye contact; they were already looking at him. Now they wanted the man to look back at them: "Then Peter said, 'Look at us!' So the man gave them his attention, expecting to get something from them. But Peter said, 'I have no silver and gold, but what I do have I give to you; in the name of Jesus Christ of Nazareth rise up and walk" (Acts 3:4–6).

The man's hope was to get some sort of material possession, right? According to the Jesus Method, Peter and John had this moment with a guest, which means the next step was providing for him. Notice, however, provision isn't always what the guests think they need; provision is what God has given you to give to them. In this case, what the man needed was something outside of his previous life experience. What he really needed could not be found by studying himself or his past experiences more deeply; it could only come from God. It was healing, and that healing led to walking and leaping and praising God, making him a great witness of Jesus. Peter and John, on the other hand, simply listened to and obeyed what the Spirit was wanting to do and left the consequences up to God.

> Provision isn't always what the guests think they need; provision is what God has given you to give to them.

Those consequences soon had the two of them in front of the high council—another dilemma! The high council was made up of individuals who claimed to be a part of the family. Let's watch how the Holy Spirit guided Peter through the Jesus Method.

> Then Peter, filled with the Holy Spirit, said to them: "Rulers and elders of the people! If we are being called to account today for an act of kindness shown to a man who was lame and are being asked how he was healed, then know this, you and all the people of Israel: It is by the name of Jesus Christ of Nazareth, whom you crucified but whom God raised from the dead, that this man stands before you healed. Jesus is 'the stone you builders rejected, which has become the cornerstone.' Salvation is found in no one else, for there is no other name under heaven given to mankind by which we must be saved." (Acts 4:8–12 NIV)

Since the council claimed to be a part of the family, and since this was already in a personal setting, the Holy Spirit directly challenged them with truth. This challenge was a very bold witness, and their boldness surprised the high council. Remember that God is big enough to work on everyone in every situation. Peter and John were in the family, so the Holy Spirit was also challenging them to be bold in their obedience to God's strategy of being a witness while empowering them with exactly what they needed to say. The council didn't know what to do about all of this, so they threatened them to not ever speak about this again, thus showing their cards that they were indeed guests trying to use power to spread fear. Continuing to listen and obey and leaving the consequences to God, Peter and John gave their now famous response: "But Peter and John replied, 'Which is right in God's eyes: to listen to you, or to him? You be the judges! As for us, we cannot help speaking about what we have seen and heard'" (Acts 4:19–20). They had provided the truth about salvation, which is what those guests needed, and the guests chose to not accept it. So Peter and John respected their choice and walked away, but they did not stop being a witness to what they had *seen and heard.*

Did you catch that last part? They walked away but kept on being witnesses for Christ. Many of the social dilemmas we face will not result in everyone agreeing. Trying to force that agreement will likely lead us down the wrong path of overemphasizing right and wrong and powering up in some way. That being said, disagreement does not mean we must be silent about Jesus. We are to continue to be witnesses for Christ and in the way Jesus modeled.

Another good example of the Holy Spirit following the Jesus Method happens in Acts 5. It's a tragic story but one that confirms the process. Two people, Ananias and Sapphira, claimed to be family but secretly refused to follow the will of the Father:

> A man named Ananias, with the consent of his wife Sapphira, sold a piece of property and with his wife's knowledge he kept back for himself some of the proceeds and brought only a part of it and laid it at the apostles' feet. Peter said, "Ananias, why has Satan filled your heart to lie to the Holy Spirit to keep back for yourself part of the proceeds of the land? While it remained unsold, did it not remain your own? And after it was

sold, was it not at your own disposal? Why is it that you have contrived this deed in your heart? You've not lied to man but to God." When Ananias heard these words he fell down and breathed his last, and great fear came upon all who heard it. The young men rose and wrapped him up and carried him out and buried him. (Acts 5:1–5)

He claimed to be family, and so the Holy Spirit, through Peter, challenged Ananias in a family conversation. Soon it became clear that he was a guest and had already filled his heart with a plan of selfish gain, like the deceiving guests in Jude. There was no longer a heart dilemma in Ananias. He had chosen to form his truth from his experience of what would be best. Peter respected that decision and did not try to change his mind. Peter did not argue nor retaliate, and he did not take it upon himself to enact punishment. He left the consequences of Ananias's spiritual decision (and then Sapphira's as well) to God. Unfortunately for them, tragic consequences came quickly.

No matter how blatant or clear the offense is that is causing the social dilemma, we are to trust God with the discipline of those guests. In our own lives we are likely to be white-hot mad at certain moments during social dilemmas, but emotions should never outweigh the example of Jesus. Never. No matter the sin. No step in the Jesus Method agrees with, accepts, or tolerates sin, but the goal is always relationship. When that goal is no longer reachable with guests, we must turn them and the consequences of their spiritual choices over to God. Our process is done. We let them go with no retaliation, no fighting, and no demands for explanation. Oh, our heart may be completely crushed in that moment, as I'm sure Peter's was, but that is what Jesus modeled in his method. All of this takes an incredible amount of self-control, which is why we need to live in dependence on God through his Spirit.

Some of us are exhausted in our social dilemmas because we are trying to control all the outcomes. We're afraid of what might happen if we say or do certain things wrong, and we're afraid of what might happen if we don't say anything at all. We need to follow the method of Jesus and then fully hand over the rest for God to handle. I know this is easier said than done, but there is a peace that comes from following through on the Jesus Method. We can trust that God will do whatever he knows is best for all those involved.

Another powerful social dilemma in the book of Acts involves a very loud and powerful guest who met face to face with Jesus. We might encounter some of these people in our social dilemmas too. In Acts 9, we find the precocious Saul of Tarsus on a zealous rampage that supposedly was for God. In one of the best examples of a full-blown misunderstanding of contending for the faith, Saul hunted down people who had seemingly wrong beliefs. He believed that God wanted him to deal out consequences for their spiritual decisions, which Saul thought was part of contending for the faith. He trusted in the power that he had been given to persecute those who were wrong and to spread fear to others who may be a part of the so-called way of Jesus. Obviously, this is pretty much the opposite of the Jesus Method. Seeking power, Saul made things very public. We get a glimpse of the state of Saul's heart when a follower of Jesus, Stephen, was martyred after being a bold witness of Jesus (Acts 7). Saul's heart wasn't pretty. He definitely didn't have the goal of relationship, and he seemed obsessed with playing God's role in issuing punishment.

Then Saul and Jesus had a showdown on the road to Damascus, and Jesus once again modeled his method. Not surprisingly, Jesus opened with a question. We often see Jesus approach people in his method with questions. This is helpful in our lives as well. Seeking to hear more of someone's story by asking questions is a good way to start relationship. Jesus knew that dialogue has a much better opportunity to lead to relationship than simply giving answers or issuing commands: "He fell to the ground and heard a voice say to him, 'Saul, Saul, why do you persecute me?' 'Who are you, Lord?' Saul asked. 'I am Jesus, whom you are persecuting,' he replied. 'Now get up and go into the city, and you will be told what you must do'" (Acts 9:4–6 NIV).

The heart of Saul was in a dilemma, and Jesus met him right there. Jesus came to Saul face to face because he cared about Saul, so he made it personal. Saul claimed to be in the family, so Jesus challenged him with truth. Jesus followed his witness strategy of identifying himself as God with an "I AM" statement. Saul accepted the truth and was empowered with next steps in his relationship with God. At the same time, God was challenging a man already in the family named Ananias to go and meet Saul. Ananias chose to listen to and obey God's will, regardless of the fear he had about who Saul was, and his relationship with God grew. Ananias refused to give into the temptation of experience-based truth, and instead, he trusted God's truth.

Both men accepted the challenge. God empowered Ananias with healing Saul, and God empowered Saul to become Paul, the apostle to the Gentiles. Notice the one-relationship-at-a-time pace that Jesus took in this story. First with Saul, then with Ananias, and then Saul with Ananias, God was growing relationship with each of them and with each other. That's a much more pleasant ending to this story than in Acts 5, but it's the same process being fulfilled in both. The ending of these stories depends on the choices that the people made within the stories. Jesus's method is consistent, but human hearts are not. It is important for us to remember that we are not in charge of the end result, only in faithfully following the Jesus Method.

The next social dilemma we'll discuss pertains to how we can expect people to react as we engage them in the Jesus Method. Paul was well into his ministry at this point, and he was fully engaging in social dilemmas.

> As Paul and Barnabas were leaving the synagogue, the people invited them to speak further about these things on the next Sabbath. When the congregation was dismissed, many of the Jews and devout converts to Judaism followed Paul and Barnabas, who talked with them and urged them to continue in the grace of God. On the next Sabbath almost the whole city gathered to hear the word of the Lord. When the Jews saw the crowds, they were filled with jealousy. They began to contradict what Paul was saying and heaped abuse on him. (Acts 13:42–45 NIV)

Paul and Barnabas were providing for the spiritual needs of the crowd, inviting them into further relationship with Jesus. However, certain Jewish guests did not have relationship as their goal. They were jealous, had unbelief, and decided to choose selfish gain by navigating this social dilemma according to the ways of the world.

Using power and fear, they stirred up the crowd. They seem to have been pretty good at that sort of thing. Interestingly, in all of scripture, we never see Jesus or his disciples intentionally stirring up a crowd. That's what people who are seeking power do. They make things public to gain powerful momentum. That's the way of the world, which is far from the supernatural way of Jesus. The way of Jesus is always about inviting people into relationship. Paul and Barnabas were going to finish up the Jesus Method by sharing the gospel, which provided for the spiritual needs of the Gentile guests, and then they would respect the spiritual choices that people make.

Meanwhile, the Jewish guests doubled down on their worldly efforts. They tried to persuade more people to come to their side; incited the crowd even more; and then threatened, persecuted, and kicked out Paul and Barnabas for not thinking the same way they did. However, Paul and Barnabas respected their decision and moved on (Acts 13:46–52). We see no demeaning, belittling, or mocking comments in response. Interestingly, neither man was directly a part of the training that Jesus did with his disciples, but the Holy Spirit in them carried on the Jesus Method perfectly. They shook off the dust from their feet and moved on. The goal is relationship through the strategy of being a witness. The gospel was "spreading through the whole region," and the Gentiles rejoiced in their opportunity for relationship with God.

This dilemma in the early church is a great reminder for us today. Not everyone is going to accept Jesus, and even though we care for and love those individuals just as much as anyone else, we cannot let their "no" steal the joy from our hearts. Just like Paul and Barnabas, God does not intend us to engage every argument, debate, or conflict. We provide for the guests, and when they do not want Jesus, we can have joy in moving on to the next opportunity God brings. For me this can feel like quitting in some way on God, but that's not true. Rather, we are obeying him and quitting on the ways of the world.

This whole passage is remarkable for another reason as well. When we look back and compare Saul (guest) versus Paul (family), we notice that his conversion to Jesus didn't only change what he believed. It also changed how he lived out what he believed. The *how* changed. He now walked away with joy, not hunting down in anger. Paul's new mission required a new method, a new approach, a new *how*. He didn't just believe something new and use his old way of doing things. Paul did not hunt down, threaten, and persecute people who refused to believe in Jesus like he did as a guest. No, he was in the family now. Believing in Jesus brought a whole new way of engaging social dilemmas.

> *We notice that his conversion to Jesus didn't only change what he believed. It also changed how he lived out what he believed.*

This conversion reminds me of something that I grew up doing every single year: a yearly conversion from the soccer field to the basketball court. I loved both of these sports so much, but they were played very differently. When I was switching from soccer in the fall to basketball in the winter, I couldn't play basketball the same way I played soccer. When the coach said, "Work on dribbling and shooting the basketball," I couldn't go around kicking the ball at other players or the basket. I wouldn't have gotten to play for very long! It wasn't just a new set of rules to learn, it was a different way of playing. Offenses and defenses were different. The flow of the game was different with time-outs, free throws, and breaks at the quarters. You get the idea. When we choose to follow Jesus, it doesn't just change *what* we think is right and wrong, it changes the *way* we live. It's a different flow and process all together. We can't live as family using the same methods and processes that we used as guests. It's a different game now, with a different goal.

The goal for the family is not winning the argument. The goal for the family is not convincing everyone of what is right and wrong, or even trying to persuade everyone to follow Jesus. The goal of the family is not to correct all wrong behavior. We can't correct someone into connection with Jesus; they have to choose it. The goal of the family is not to have a show of power. The goal of the family is inviting people into a growing relationship with God, one relationship at a time. As part of the family, I believe our greatest challenge is not our inability to convince someone to follow Jesus; it's our inability to inspire someone with our own lives to want to follow Jesus. It's not about persuading someone to change their life; it's about bringing them to Jesus, who will change their life. Each person gets to choose whether they want it. Are we re-presenting Jesus well with how we engage social dilemmas? We must follow the Jesus Method the best we can. When people don't want him, we move on with respect, because fighting back never achieves the goal of relationship.

> I believe our greatest challenge is not our inability to convince someone to follow Jesus; it's our inability to inspire someone with our own lives to want to follow Jesus. It's not about persuading someone to change their life; it's about bringing them to Jesus, who will change their life.

One of my favorite stories about the Holy Spirit guiding someone through the Jesus Method happens in Acts 16. Paul was imprisoned, and instead of being angry about it, he sang hymns. He knew that what comes out of your mouth is an overflow of your heart (Luke 6:45). When you and I are pressed down or when we're in crisis, whatever is in us at the core *will* come out. It might be really ugly, or it might be really beautiful—we don't always know until we're squeezed at that level. Paul's core was full of praise as he sang songs of rejoicing. Of course, he had to have minded them in the first place to be reminded of them. It's a good reminder for us that we can only pour out what we are filled up with.

Here he was in shackles and chains. He had been put there by the jailer, whom we can assume was probably not the most kind and gentle person. All of a sudden, the shackles miraculously fell off of Paul. God is way more powerful than the strongest power of mankind. Paul was free to get out of there as fast as he could. Now, there's a social dilemma brewing, which means the goal is now relationship, not freedom from jail. You see, the jailer, who had likely caused so much pain to Paul and who represented a culture that persecuted family so aggressively, was about to kill himself because if the prisoners escaped, he would be killed. Paul could leave; it was his choice. What would the Jesus Method say to do? Paul was in the family, so the Holy Spirit challenged and empowered him. Paul's goal was not revenge or retaliation, not freedom from jail; it was freedom for the jailor and that he would have a restored relationship with God. It's the same with us, even with a person who has caused us suffering and pain. We might not know what the outcome will be, but we are responsible for providing the invitation to our enemies for a right relationship with God.

Paul knew beyond a shadow of a doubt what his goal was. He needed to provide for the spiritual needs of this man by introducing him to Jesus and inviting him into relationship. The steps of the Jesus Method couldn't have been clearer, regardless of what Paul had experienced. He acted on the truth he had received from God. It was time to listen and obey to what God had called him to do. He had already spent all night singing and praying to God through song. He was ready. Since delayed obedience is disobedience, he sat down immediately and had a conversation with the jailer. Notice the pace of one relationship at a time. There was no show of power, only a display of mercy. Sure enough, the jailer chose to accept Jesus as his savior, and then as crazy as it sounds, Paul followed the jailer to his house and his whole household went all-in for Jesus and were baptized!

Peter had a similar situation with a Roman commanding officer named Cornelius earlier in Acts 10. God gave Peter three visions of unclean food, but in the vision, God told Peter to eat the food.

Peter, wanting to defend what he knew was right and wrong, told God no. You can sense how strong right and wrong was in Peter at that moment. Even when God asked him to do something very specific, he refused to do it because it would violate what he had known to be wrong. God just warming him up because he needed to remind Peter that relationship is always the goal, not Peter's previous experience and knowledge of good and evil. Peter obeyed beyond understanding and went to Cornelius's house, which was full of Gentile guests who were supposedly unclean. Peter provided for the spiritual needs of Cornelius and his whole family, and they all were baptized! This would have been absolutely mind-blowing for Peter to take in, but that's indicative of how important relationship is to God in the Jesus Method. Just like he did for Peter, God wants his whole family to understand his goal and act on it in every social dilemma.

I wonder how often we in the church today miss God's opportunities like Peter almost did. God wants his family to be carriers of his reconciliation to people whom we might have always thought to be wrong. Before moving on in this book, take a moment to check in with God to make sure you are not missing his will being done.

As we come back to Paul in Acts 17, we see the Jesus Method continuing to be implemented by the Holy Spirit. Paul engaged the Greeks. Some believed in Epicureanism, which was a form of hedonism. Some were Stoics, which focused on virtue and what was morally right and wrong. Paul talked to these guests, providing for their spiritual needs and relating to them so that God could meet them right where they were. The reactions to Paul's invitation to have a relationship with God are representative of what typically happens today as well. Some of the guests believe, some of them laugh it off, and some of them are curious and want to know more. Paul let those who didn't believe walk away, and he spent relationship-building time with those that truly want it. He spent his limited TEAM on those who desired relationship instead of some sort of retaliatory measures on those who disagreed.

For us today, we need to know that even as we execute the Jesus Method, we will experience similar results to Paul's. Some people will respond with incredible gratitude for how our obedience to the Jesus Method is opening relationship with God. Some people simply won't be open to that, and that's OK. Unfortunately, one of the hardest things about this entire process for me is that I've had to become better at walking away from people or letting them walk away from me. These are the people who don't want to take a step toward relationship with God. However, God is always challenging me in every single situation, empowering me to stay true to the Jesus Method. Honestly, most of the time, people expect me as a pastor to be angry, retaliate, or make a big public display of my opinion. When I don't, it often opens a great dialogue where I can come alongside, have empathy and compassion, and in doing so, be provision in their life. It doesn't always lead to a conversation about Jesus in that moment. I'm OK with that. Jesus healed a bunch of guests and fed thousands of guests, and not all of them chose to be in relationship with him. That did not stop him from providing for them, and it did not change how he respected their decisions of faith. He left the consequences of the guests' choices up to his heavenly Father. I want to be content in doing the same.

I'd like to close this chapter praying for all of us.

God, I ask that you continue to work on us. Continue your sanctifying work, please. None of us have arrived. We're all arriving, and you're leading and we're following, so, Lord, if there is any conviction, any gentle reminder of what's true that you want to put on our hearts right now, please do that. Lord, with gratitude and humility we acknowledge your presence and are thankful for your wisdom. Is there anything you want to share with us right now from what we've read in this chapter that is a helpful step? Maybe it's a particular person with whom we need to have a conversation? Maybe it's asking someone to forgive us for how we've treated them? Maybe, God, you're nudging us that we need your forgiveness on something that we've never spoken about out loud, but we feel in our heart that judgment, the speck that we just can't help but see in someone else's eye? God, maybe we need your grace to wash over us? God, maybe it's an unsettledness in our spirit, that we're not sure if we agree with all of this completely and we just need to keep diving into relationship with you? Lord, I know that you have more to show us, and so, God, please help us take steps to get closer to you and to continue to wrestle with the Jesus Method. God, as we engage you with all of this, I really believe we are staying close to you, which is always a good place to be. We love you and we trust you. In Jesus's mighty name we pray, amen.

Prayerful Reflection

1. What are any new insights that God is putting on your heart about this chapter?
2. What is God challenging you in right now?
3. What is he empowering in you right now?
4. Who is he putting on your heart to challenge and empower?
5. Who is he putting on your heart to provide for and respect?

CHAPTER 8

Q & A

After discussing this topic in a lot of different settings, I thought it would be helpful to go through a few of the common questions I get. The questions and my answers are not comprehensive, but they would be my typical responses if I was in a conversation with someone face to face. I hope that you feel more equipped to answer similar questions you might receive as you engage the Jesus Method in your own life.

There are several instances in Scripture where Jesus talks about bringing a sword (Matthew 10) and bringing division (John 12:51). How does that line up with his concern for unity in John 17?

Great question—thanks for asking. Jesus prayed for unity in John 17. That is his hope, and his efforts always tried to provide that opportunity of relationship and unity with God and each other; however, the reality is he knew that his presence as a light in the darkness (John 1:5) would bring division because the darkness will try and overcome it. Many people don't want what Jesus wants (John 1:11). After all, he is the stone that the builders rejected that will become the cornerstone (Matt. 21:42). So, the division he brought is what inevitably happened, but his hope and goal was still for unity.

What about the whole flipping tables thing, though? That seemed retaliatory.

Great question—thanks for asking. I know it may seem that way, but it was completely initiated by Jesus in order to fulfill a prophecy concerning him. He was not reacting in the middle of an argument or fighting back in a particular social dilemma situation at all. In fact, he was fighting *for* the ability of Gentiles to have an unrivaled relationship with God. This area was the closest to the presence of God Gentiles were allowed to be on the temple grounds. He was clearing the space for the Gentiles to be able to meet with God, instead of being deceived by those there for selfish gain or being distracted by supposedly having the right sacrifice or giving the right amount of offering. He wanted to reestablish the priority of the heart of worship over the misaligned priority of what is right and wrong in the Law.

What about how Jesus spoke to the Pharisees? He called them white-washed tombs, sons of the devil and snakes. That doesn't seem like he respected their spiritual choices.

Great question—thanks for asking. I get it, and it certainly doesn't seem that way, does it? I'll admit that these are moments when I believe that Jesus had perfect discernment of their hearts, and he knew that relationship was not currently an option. Most importantly, as you read these accounts, you'll notice that Jesus said these things as warnings to others listening in. In other words, he still respected the Pharisees' spiritual choices because he was not

fighting directly with the religious leaders in a retaliatory way, trying to bully them into the truth or persuade them to change their
minds. I believe he responded like this in order to fulfill what Jude
talks about: trying to snatch those in the crowd who were heading
toward the same fiery consequences as those religious leaders. Yes,
it is strong language. I believe he used it with hopes of providing
clarity to the other guests listening in or to those in the family who
were tempted to follow the religious leaders. Even still, he never
enacted any punitive measures, mocked them, or physically hurt
them, though he did point to the consequences that were coming
someday. Remember, that is still part of the Jesus Method: leaving
them to God, who judges justly. Personally, even though we see
Jesus do this a few times, I stay away from any sort of strong language. Unlike Jesus, I know that I do not have perfect discernment
of people's hearts. The Holy Spirit is at work fully now, and I'm
trusting him to carry the load of convicting others (John 16:7–11).

**How do you stay focused on relationship when you're so
frustrated or disappointed?**

Great question—thanks for asking. I love that you assume I get
frustrated and disappointed, because I totally do! Personally, I
remind myself that a questioner is behind the question and that
God's goal is always relationship. God loves that person even more
than I do, so the most loving thing I can do is to follow the Jesus
Method. Other than that, I make sure to stay locked in on listening
to God as I navigate the conversation or situation. I also take time to
pray with God about the grief I feel about it all. Being sad and disappointed is not weakness. Those emotions are evidence that I really
care about the person or the situation. God always welcomes those
times together to process the heartache. I have also developed a bit

of a mantra in times like these. It sounds like this: "I'm a Christian, so I do hard things. That's what I do because that's what Jesus did."

What's my responsibility to hold the ones I love, including family members, accountable?

Great question—thanks for asking. As parents, I believe that we have a tremendous responsibility to train our kids in the ways of the Lord (Prov. 22:6). We must disciple them as Jesus did (we can talk more about that some other time because it's a big topic), but you asked specifically about "accountability." What does that word mean to you?

- I let them respond, and usually their answer has a focus on making sure the ones they love believe the right things and do the right things.
- Then I ask, "Is there a particular dilemma you're in right now that you're willing to share about, just so I can answer your question more specifically?"
- I let them respond again, and this is where the Holy Spirit really starts to move. All of a sudden, I have the opportunity to sit with them in a vulnerable space, which opens up relationship. More often than not, they share about an addiction, unbelief, or sexual immorality.
- I then go on to share two things: First, your responsibility is to follow the Jesus Method (and we might work together to figure out the next step to take). Second, I usually ask, "Does this person you care about know what you believe? Are they clear on that?" Almost always their response is something like, "Oh yeah—they're clear!" OK, so they're clear on what you believe is true, but do they know that you love them? That you still want relationship with them? I'm

sure if they change their mind or want to debate, they know how to get a hold of you, but I think part of your responsibility is to help them know that you are willing to still walk beside them. This doesn't mean you agree. I'm sure you've made that clear. They get that, but they may not be getting that you still care about them. Remember, caring is not condoning. They may be confused on whether you are willing to walk beside them through this challenge.

- I definitely always want to close out this particular question with prayer, in case God wants to challenge them specifically with something, which happens quite often.

How do you get the most bang for your buck being a witness?

Great question—thanks for asking. I would try to make God as normal as possible in your everyday life. Smash your normal life and your faith completely together. For example, when a guest asks you about your weekend, you can talk about things you did and then share how you heard some truth at church that really encouraged you. You can be more specific if you want, and then, without stopping or making a huge deal about it, keep talking about other things you did over the weekend. Another thing that's important to focus on is identity. When you share with a guest or family member about how you are experiencing God, make sure to emphasize *who* God is, not just what he does. People are naturally tempted to let their experience determine their truth, which seems fine when their experiences in life are going well. They will think God must be good. What happens, though, when they're experiencing bad things in life? They will think God must be bad. Do you see? Experience-based truth is really deceiving. So when you share about God, make sure you prioritize *who* he is over *what* he has done, and then *who* he has made you to be over *what* you get to do for him. Sharing about all of it is important, but the order is extremely important.

How do you handle sustained conflict in social dilemmas when someone keeps coming at you?

Great question—thanks for asking. My first step is to pray to make sure that God is wanting me to walk away. If he wants me to keep engaging the Jesus Method, then I do, trying to exhibit the fruit of the Spirit. If God does want me to walk away, I try to have a personal conversation with the individual where I say something like this: "I appreciate that you've engaged me in conversation about this topic. I love that you haven't let awkwardness prevent relationship and dialogue; well done. We've been able to ask each other questions, share our thoughts, and challenge one other. I've appreciated your openness and transparency. It's clear to me that we are not going to agree on this particular issue, and that's OK. I don't believe any further conversation is going to change that. That being said, I'd love to pray together, if you're up for that, and then we can go on our way."

What about church discipline?

Great question—thanks for asking. Church discipline is a very specific subset of the Jesus Method. Church discipline is a way of challenging the family into restored relationship with God. With that heart for restored relationship as my goal, I fully follow the model Jesus laid out in Matthew 18. What you'll notice as you engage that method is that it syncs up perfectly with the Jesus Method. It's one relationship at a time, where the crucial conversations are very personal, with just a few people involved, and those conversations challenge the person as family. However, if they don't respond to those challenges with a desire to restore relationship with God, treat them as a guest. Now, we are launched back into the full Jesus Method where we pray, provide, and respect their spiritual choices.

Why are Christians so angry?

Great question—thanks for asking. I've heard a pastor friend of mine introduce himself as "a conservative evangelical in the Wesleyan tradition, and I'm not angry about it." People always laugh because they sense in the church culture exactly what you're asking about. Christians seem angry, and pastors seem *really* angry. In all seriousness, though, if you have ever been hurt by a Christian who is angry, I want to say that I'm sorry about that. Unfortunately, we don't always re-present an accurate picture of Christ, and that's on us—it's not who Jesus is. Back to your question, I honestly think many Christians are angry because for years they've felt bullied by the enemy and the world. During all that time, they've never been equipped to do anything about it. It's like a kid who gets bullied at school and then finally hits a growth spurt and wants to fight back. It's a natural response, but it's not Jesus's *supernatural* response. By and large, Christians have only been equipped either to fight back in worldly ways or remain silent and stay out of it. This is why I'm talking about this so much, and it's why I wrote this book! God wants to equip us with a whole different method, one that focuses on relationship above everything else.

What about civic situations (including politics)?

Great question—thanks for asking. I know that many situations happening in our schools, cities, states, and federal government platforms are concerning you. I can tell by the passion in your question. I love that! When it comes to politics, I vote my faith, and if I am asked, I share with others according to the context of relationship. I also support those whom I see genuinely advocating for others with the heart of Jesus. However, I do not put my hope and trust in any governmental institutions. I just don't see Jesus doing that. The same goes for other civic organizations. I strictly operate within the Jesus Method, as people or situations approach me. Currently, my impact circles are not connected to civic organizations in this way. However, I can see how some people are called to pursue the Jesus Method in those contexts. As long as relationship with God and others is truly the goal of their heart and they're willing to engage the Jesus Method thoroughly, I think God could use them in powerful ways.

What about apologetics? That seems like we are trying to defend something, doesn't it?

Great question—thanks for asking. I love apologetics because the whole idea of it comes straight from scripture (1 Pet. 3:15 ESV). Let's look at that verse right now: "But in your hearts honor Christ the Lord as holy, always being prepared to make a defense to anyone who asks you for a reason for the hope that is in you; yet do it with gentleness and respect."

The first step that the older and wiser Peter laid out for us is to revere Christ in our hearts as Lord, which sounds just like what we were talking about in Jude. Contending for the faith starts with strengthening our own relationship with Christ, which might include a log or two that needs to be removed! With that established, we engage the Jesus Method. There is someone who has a question about our faith, and we get to provide for them. What are we providing? A defense for the hope that we have in Jesus.

Emphasis here is placed on our *hope*. People forget that sometimes and try to replace "hope" with "right doctrinal belief." I get it. Sure, our hope comes from what we believe to be true, but the emphasis is on hope in this verse. Note also that regardless of how they receive our hope defense, we do this kindly and are full of respect for the individual and whatever choices they eventually make. If they are a family member, we can challenge them with kindness and respect, of course, so it fits quite well into the Jesus Method.

Those are some of the FAQ's I've gotten speaking on this topic. I hope they were helpful to you. I also hope that this book has equipped you to know Jesus modeled another way to cross the traffic of our social dilemmas. I pray that you courageously engage further conversation with God on questions such as these: *What do I do with this? Is there someone in my impact circle with whom I should build relationship? What's my next step when I think about the goal of relationship and my witness?* These are helpful questions to kick-start more conversations with God. I'm proud of you for engaging this material with me. I'm sure some of it has challenged you like it's challenged me! I'd love to close our time together in prayer:

Heavenly Father, I ask that whatever people have felt, whatever they have thought, whatever they have agreed with or disagreed with, that your salvation—what Jesus has done for us—will somehow unify your people and your church, just as Jesus prayed. I know we're going to disagree with each other on certain things, and I know there's going to be messiness. God, I pray that our relationship with you grounds us and unifies us that we might be a witness of you wherever we are in whatever we are doing. I ask that people would love you and love each other the way you have loved us. We need your help in this, Lord. Guide us and help us navigate all our social dilemmas in your way, Jesus. Now, as we close our time together, please give each of us the courage to say yes to whatever you're asking us to do with what we've learned. Empower us to be your witness. We love you and we trust you. In Jesus's name we pray, amen.

SCAN HERE to learn more about Invite Press, a premier publishing imprint created to invite people to a deeper faith and living relationship with Jesus Christ.

Printed in the USA
CPSIA information can be obtained
at www.ICGtesting.com
CBHW030554280324
5965CB00005B/16